Optimising your academic career:
Advice for early career scholars

Optimising your academic career: Advice for early career scholars

Carol Mutch

NZCER PRESS

NZCER PRESS
New Zealand Council for Educational Research
PO Box 3237
Wellington
New Zealand

www.nzcer.org.nz

© Carol Mutch 2017

ISBN: 978-0-947509-75-0

No part of the publication may be copied, stored or communicated in any form by any means (paper or digital), including recording or storing in an electronic retrieval system, without the written permission of the publisher.
Education institutions that hold a current licence with Copyright Licensing New Zealand may copy from this book in strict accordance with the terms of the CLNZ Licence.

A catalogue record for this book is available from the National Library of New Zealand.

Designed by Smartwork Creative Ltd

Contents

Preface	vii
Chapter 1 Becoming an academic	**1**
What is an academic?	2
What is expected of an early career academic?	4
Why do people become academics?	5
What are the benefits?	5
Chapter 2 Securing a position	**7**
What are tertiary institutions looking for?	7
How can you position yourself to be considered for an academic position?	8
What is a typical recruitment process for an early career academic?	10
What is expected in an application for an early career academic position?	11
What happens in a typical appointment process?	12
Does everyone have an equal chance?	14
Chapter 3 Developing your niche	**15**
What can you expect before you start?	15
What can you learn from reflecting on your career to date?	17
How might you envision your academic future?	17
How do you describe your area of expertise?	18
How and when do you say yes or no to opportunities?	18
How do you keep your focus?	19
Chapter 4 Planning your career pathway	**20**
What is your ultimate goal?	20
What are some useful considerations along the way?	21
What other responsibilities might make calls on your time?	23
What other opportunities might present themselves?	24
What is important in the end?	25
Chapter 5 Finding a mentor	**26**
What is a mentor?	26
Are there different kinds of mentors?	27
How do you find a mentor?	29
Should you participate in a formal mentoring programme?	30
What might you expect from a mentor?	30
Chapter 6 Becoming a tutor or teaching assistant	**32**
Why undertake tutoring?	32
How do you make tutorials worthwhile?	33
How might you structure your tutorials?	36
What is your role in preparing students for assignments and examinations?	37
How do you prepare a teaching portfolio?	40

Chapter 7 **Developing your teaching**	42
How do you gain teaching experience?	42
What do you need to know about undergraduate teaching?	43
How do you incorporate skill development?	45
What do you need to know about postgraduate teaching?	46
What is culturally responsive teaching?	48
How might you teach in more innovative formats?	51
Chapter 8 **Building a research platform**	54
How do you use your earlier work as a platform for developing your research trajectory?	54
How do you go about seeking funding for new or future research?	56
How do you go about seeking funding for new or future research?	57
What is expected in a research funding proposal (RFP)?	58
How do you keep up your research momentum?	60
Chapter 9 **Organising a writing plan**	61
How do you maximise your earlier efforts?	61
What do you include in an abstract?	64
How do you set up a writing plan?	64
How do you keep up writing momentum?	66
Chapter 10 **Preparing for publication**	69
How do you get published?	69
How do you turn your thesis into a book?	71
How do you choose your dissemination outlets carefully?	73
How do you determine authorship?	76
What is a typical publishing process?	76
How do you cope with rejection?	77
Chapter 11 **Undertaking supervisions**	80
Why is supervision important?	81
What are the personal and professional benefits of research supervision?	82
What is expected of you as a supervisor?	83
How do you work with students whose backgrounds are different to your own?	86
What do you do when issues arise?	87
What is involved in examining theses and dissertations?	88
Chapter 12 **Engaging in service**	91
What is service?	92
How do you contribute at a collegial level?	93
What is expected at a departmental or institutional level?	93
What can you do in the service of your discipline?	94
How do you offer service to your profession?	95
How can you engage in community service?	96

Chapter 13 Seminars and conferences	**98**
Why is attending and participating in seminars important?	98
What can you gain from attending and presenting at conferences?	99
How do you give a professional presentation?	102
How do you engage in networking and follow up?	103
Should you publish in conference proceedings?	103
Chapter 14 Preparing for continuation and promotion	**105**
How do you make the most of your time prior to tenure?	105
How do you prepare for confirmation or continuation?	107
How do you prepare your evidence portfolio?	107
What is the place of your teaching portfolio?	109
How are different cultural approaches taken into consideration?	109
What do you need to do to be ready to apply for promotion?	110
Chapter 15 Disseminating your research more widely	**113**
How do you increase your academic uptake?	113
How do you spread your ideas more widely?	115
How do you influence policy and practice?	117
How do you engage with the media?	118
How do you exercise your critic and conscience role?	119
Chapter 16 Developing your leadership	**120**
What is meant by leadership capabilities?	120
How do you develop leadership in teaching?	122
How do you develop leadership in research?	123
How do you develop leadership *in* and *through* service?	124
What is the place of collaborative leadership?	125
Chapter 17 Managing the demands	**127**
What can you expect in your first few years?	127
How do you fit it all in?	130
How do you maintain a life outside academia?	133
Where do you go for help?	135
Chapter 18 Setting up your own Emerging Scholars Forum	**138**
How do you find out what is already available?	138
How do you determine if there is interest in forming your own group?	139
How do you set up an Emerging Scholars Forum?	140
Notes	143
References	144
Index	145

Preface

Titiro whakamuri, kokiri whakamua

Look back and reflect so you can move forward

I first entered academia in Aotearoa New Zealand in 1989 on a short-term contract as a lecturer. I have witnessed many changes since then—mergers and restructurings, a rapid growth of private training institutions, the introduction of the Tertiary Education Commission, the arrival of the Performance-Based Research Fund (PBRF) and the neoliberalising of the sector. I have felt the shift from a high trust model to a results-based accountability framework. I have seen the support that administrative staff once gave to academics moved to a centralised service that focuses more on the needs of the institution. While I still get great satisfaction from the work I do, I can see that there are increasing stresses on my newer colleagues as they navigate the demands of a world different to the one in which I began my academic career.

In 2014, in response to recently appointed colleagues and doctoral candidates asking me for advice, I set up my first Emerging Scholars Forum. I thought that rather than giving the same advice to a range of different individuals, I would get them all together. They could not only ask me for advice and but also learn from each other. Giving advice was not something I was new to. In all the institutions where I have worked I have taken my role as a mentor seriously. As well as working with individuals, I have run numerous workshops on conducting research, writing for publication, supervising postgraduate students and examining theses. Over time, I have been invited to other tertiary institutions to help set up their research culture or to conferences to run workshops on research methods and academic writing. Some of this advice has been included in one of my earlier books, *Doing Educational Research* (Mutch, 2005/2013). Recently, I was invited to speak to emerging academics at another university. After this session, one of the participants wrote:

> Thank you so, so much for yesterday. The session was so well received—people were 'buzzing' when I came back from lunch. A number of people mentioned how valuable the niche statement exercise was. Your examples of a research plan and how to link research with teaching were also extremely useful—people were having conversations about working collaboratively to research aspects of their teaching and were really excited by the possibilities. Most of all they commented on your really down-to-earth, realistic and rounded perspective on academia. They found it so refreshing to hear from someone who values teaching and service alongside research. Thank you! By far the best session we have had on developing an academic career.

As I put together a PowerPoint for the workshop, I went through the materials I had gathered and used for the Emerging Scholars Forum over the 3 years it had been operating. I thought it might be helpful if all this material was in one place. I conducted a literature search for similar books but found that much of the advice was out-of-date or not tailored to the New Zealand context. So here we are in 2017 with the ideas, activities, tips, discussion, and advice distilled into book form for a New Zealand audience. While the book is designed for those new to or contemplating an academic career, I hope it will also be helpful to more experienced academics who support and mentor new and emerging scholars.

I deliberately use loose terms such as 'new academics' or 'emerging scholars' because I don't want to exclude anyone. I mean new(ish) to academia; that is, holding a contract that includes the tertiary level activities of teaching, research and service and for whom a higher-level qualification, such as a doctorate, or a relevant professional qualification, is an expectation. I am aware that with the chequered history of academic institutions in New Zealand, there are many people who worked in the former colleges of education or polytechnics who are very experienced in some academic activities but newer to others. My first Emerging Scholars Forum included some of these very experienced lecturers and senior lecturers who were completing their doctorates later in their careers. I invited them to join the Forum alongside new academic appointments, doctoral candidates considering academic careers, and professional colleagues seconded from their organisations and tasting academic life for the first time. My aim was to focus on what they had in common rather than the differing pathways that brought them to their current positions.

The use of the term 'tertiary institutions' is also deliberate. This is not just for emerging academics in traditional universities but in the range of institutions of higher learning in New Zealand, including wānanga, institutes or universities of technology (polytechnics) and the range of private providers. I currently work in a university so I have sought input from colleagues in other settings to ensure this advice transfers across institutional cultures. As I work in education, I have also sought input from colleagues outside that field so that the advice crosses disciplinary boundaries.

This book is set out as a series of answers to the question: 'How do you go about …?' for example, becoming an academic, securing a position, and so on. It is roughly chronological in that decisions about becoming an academic will come before decisions about teaching or publishing but each chapter is written to be independent of the others. It is hoped that as a new academic is contemplating what to do next, they will review the advice provided in the relevant chapter to help them make a more informed decision. There is slight overlap as some advice crosses multiple aspects of a new academic's role. I have avoided provided reading lists or websites for readers to follow up. When revising *Doing Educational Research*, I became aware that the publishing and on-line world is rapidly evolving and constantly updating so no sooner would I recommend something than it is superseded by something newer.

In writing this book, I wanted the tone to be conversational. I wanted to tell readers what I had discovered on my academic journey and I wanted the voices of newer academics and their more experienced colleagues to complement my advice. I am very grateful to my colleagues at all levels of the system, to other writers I have cited, and bloggers who have generously given me permission to include their advice. Having said that, I am responsible for any comments that are not formally acknowledged, thus errors of fact, personal opinions, or contentious advice are mine alone and do not reflect the stance of my contributors or my institution.

This book was only made possible with the support of many people. First are the many early career academics who have discussed their issues and ideas with me over several decades. The establishment of the first Emerging Scholars Forum provided an opportunity to consolidate that advice. Second are the many colleagues with whom I have shared conversations, frustrations and laughter. Much of their wisdom has found its way into this book. Third, more specifically, are the early career and experienced academics whose words appear alongside the text. Most I knew personally but several I contacted after reading their blogs. Fourth are the pre-publication reviewers—Jacoba Matapo, Marek Tesar, Sophie Tauwehe Tamati and Bridget Percy. The book is all the better for your sharp eyes and thoughtful feedback. Finally, thanks again to David Ellis and the team at NZCER Press—you make the process from submission to publication so easy.

Carol Mutch
June 2017

Chapter 1 Becoming an academic

Whāia te iti kahurangi ki te tūohu koe me he maunga teitei
Seek the treasure you value most dearly: if you bow your head, let it be to a lofty mountain

- What is an academic?
- What is expected of an early career academic?
- Why do people become academics?
- What are the benefits?

You are probably reading this book because you are considering a career in academia. You might have preconceived ideas about what academia is and what academics do. In fact, the role can vary widely, depending on the institution, the tasks you are expected to undertake, and the pathways available to you. Don't be fooled by public perceptions of Einstein-like figures sitting in their ivory towers mumbling incomprehensibly to themselves. The job of being an academic is hard work—perhaps not in the physical sense—but you will move between a wide variety of tasks including teaching, marking, attending meetings, conducting research, giving seminars, sitting on committees, writing articles, meeting with students, seeking research funding, presenting at conferences, conducting practical workshops or laboratories, visiting students on clinical placements, supervising research students, and examining theses—all with set deadlines and expectations of quality. It will feel sometimes as if there is never enough time to complete each of these tasks to your satisfaction. This book aims to give you a glimpse into academic life and prepare you for what to expect if this is where you see your future career. It aims to lessen your anxiety and provide advice to help you find your place in what can sometimes be a bewildering and isolating environment. It also aims to assist you to plan your career in a way that will enable you meet the personal and professional goals you have set for yourself.

There are two key messages running through the book. First, *take time to enjoy your new life*. Don't be in a hurry to tick off all the milestones and achievements. Avoid comparing yourself to others. Focus on the passion for your field that brought you into academia. Find a balance that allows you to appreciate and enjoy life inside and outside academia. After reading this book, I also hope that you have the confidence to challenge the increasingly individualistic and competitive focus of our neoliberal institutions and contribute to a more nurturing, collaborative, and inclusive intellectual environment for yourself and your colleagues.

My second message is that *academic life provides you with great privilege but also has great responsibility*. You will be in a position that has endless opportunities, high status, and good remuneration. You earn this recognition because you are charged with preparing the next generation of citizens, professionals, creators, leaders, and thinkers and because—through your teaching and scholarship—you have the chance to influence the kind of society we could become.

If we want a world that is fair and just, where people respect each other and where we can each make a difference, then you can model those attributes and promote that vision in all aspects of your new role.

> "Academic life is a privilege—enjoy it and value it."
> (GM, early career academic)

What is an academic?

You no doubt bring prior knowledge of academic institutions and the people who inhabit them to your new role. You might have fond memories of lecturers who helped you through your qualifications or not such fond memories of late nights in the library trying to meet deadlines. Whatever your experience, something has now drawn you to thinking about academia as a career.

In general, academics are people who have completed advanced degrees and work in institutions of higher learning with a scholarly or professional focus. In New Zealand, these institutions are universities, polytechnics, wānanga, and some private training organisations. In institutions such as polytechnics, 'dual professionals'—who continue to work in their industry as well as teach professional courses—may have their work experience recognised in place of advanced qualifications. In some countries, academics can choose to focus on research *or* teaching *or* administration. In New Zealand, most positions are a combination of all three aspects. The most common pattern of employment in my university is what we call a 40/40/20 role—that is, 40% teaching, 40% research and 20% service.

In many institutions, there are roles, such as Senior Tutors or Professional Teaching Fellows, who are not expected to research and there are roles, such as Research Fellows, who are not expected to teach—so there is variation within the concept of an academic position. In other countries, institutions can be more research intensive *or* more teaching intensive, but in New Zealand many institutions include both aspects. Tertiary institutions aim to employ individuals who combine the range of necessary attributes or who bring complementary expertise to cover that particular institution's needs.

There are common sets of expectations under each of the teaching, research, and service aspects of an academic's role. My university has 'academic standards' that outline what is expected at each stage of an academic's career, especially when applying for continuation or promotion. These guidelines set out what an academic can be expected to contribute to the university and to their discipline. Allowances are made for the different expectations across the three main disciplinary groupings of natural sciences, social sciences and humanities. The standards cover:

> "Generally, the career path in academia starts with a research higher degree then appointment at lecturer level progressing to senior lecturer, associate professor and then full professor. Career progression is not related to length of service, but to achievement in research, teaching, and leadership. The balance between these areas often varies over a career and between individuals. Some academics will have a research-only role, but even here they are expected to provide training and mentorship to early career researchers. Some academics will have a large teaching role, but will still be expected to publish and engage in scholarship of some form."
> (IS, senior academic)[1]

- contributions to teaching
- contributions to research, scholarship or artistic activity, and
- contributions to the university, discipline, profession and/or community.

There is more variation in roles outside the university sector, where there might be different disciplinary groupings, career pathways, and professional expectations.

What is expected of an early career academic?

As an early career academic who is newly appointed to a lecturing position, you would be expected to contribute to teaching by engaging in intellectually challenging, culturally appropriate, research-informed teaching. This might include preparing and delivering tutorials, lectures and workshops, selecting appropriate course readings and activities, preparing and grading assessments and examinations, and contributing to course planning and reviews. You do this while working within relevant policies and guidelines (see Chapters 6 and 7). You might be expected to begin supervising student projects or to join postgraduate thesis supervision teams (see Chapter 11). If you work in a professional programme, you might also be expected to contribute to activities such as conducting clinics or visiting students on placements (see Chapter 12).

Under the research category, an early career scholar would be expected to begin to build a portfolio of publications in high quality outlets, such as international peer-reviewed journals (see Chapters 9 and 10). If you have recently completed a thesis, an immediate focus might be turning your thesis into a book or series of journal articles, depending on what is most valued in your discipline. Applying for research grants from departmental or institutional sources, or external grants as part of team, could also be a key part of a new academic's role (see Chapter 8). It is important that as an early career scholar you build a sustainable research trajectory that enables you to maintain publication momentum.

"Academics are the life-blood of a university, without whom the institution would not exist." (University of Manchester website)[2]

Finally, an early career academic would be expected to display, what I term 'academic citizenship'. This means that you attend meetings, join committees, review for journals, present seminars, engage with your relevant professional, discipline, or cultural communities, and generally act in a collegial manner. As time passes, your career portfolio should extend to demonstrate your willingness to engage in leadership and mentoring (see Chapters 5 and 16).

Why people become academics

There are many reasons for becoming an academic—for some, it is a straightforward path from school to undergraduate and postgraduate study before finding an opening in a tertiary institution. For others, it is a later career decision after many years in other walks of life, gathering qualifications along the way.

For a lucky few, it is a tap on the shoulder inviting you to apply for a position and then winning it.

My own career began after many years as a practitioner to finding myself on the other side of the fence, preparing those practitioners in undergraduate and postgraduate programmes. This is a common pathway in applied fields such as education, social work, nursing and law. Many of us did not ever imagine a career in academia but we became interested in the bigger questions of our field, using higher qualifications as a way to make sense of our profession until an academic career became the next logical step.

> *"For me becoming an academic was about negotiating turbulent layers in my thinking and my desires. I surveyed the waters from ashore as an early childhood teacher and after much thinking crossed the waters to the opposite shore."* (DL, early career academic)

> *"There is no single career path into academic medicine. I was fortunate enough to go to a medical school that included a 6-month research project as part of the core curriculum and gave me my first taste for research, but it was not until I took 3 years out of my clinical training before starting work as a registrar to do my MD that knew I wanted to be an academic."* (IS, senior academic)

What are the benefits?

There are many benefits to an academic career. I have found it personally and professionally rewarding. I moved from a career as a teacher to then preparing the next generation of teachers. I can still remember the pleasure of sharing my real-life experiences with these would-be teachers. I remember the excitement of coming to grips with educational theories that helped explain why things happened as they did. I remember the thrill of conducting my first piece of research and later holding in my hands the journal that contained my first published academic article. As I was driving across the Canterbury Plains on a warm summer's day to observe a student teacher on practicum in a small rural school I said to myself, almost in disbelief, "And someone is actually paying me to do this!"

As I look back over my career, it has been a life full of opportunities and privileges. I have been able to follow up matters of social and educational importance through research, speaking, writing and teaching. I have watched with pride as my students have graduated and gone on to have significant impact on their fields. I have travelled the world to engage with colleagues with similar interests. Many academics today feel a little disillusioned with the way academia has been changed by neoliberal ideologies. When market forces influence higher education, academics tend to become more competitive in the way they teach and research, more individualistic in the way interact with colleagues and more protective as they feel the pressures of accountability encroaching on their time. I have observed these changes first-hand and one of the motivations for writing this book was to help new academics navigate their way through the complexity that is academia today yet still find the joy of engaging in trying to find answers to life's 'wicked problems'.[3]

"If you are interested in financial rewards as the main benefit of an academic career, you should probably stop reading now! The rewards of an academic career are more in terms of personal and professional satisfaction. There are opportunities to travel, to meet and work with colleagues from around the world, and, through the results of your research or leadership, to influence the future direction of the speciality. No two weeks are the same. You have the immediate satisfaction of being able to practise your craft ... combined with the excitement of new discoveries through research and the reward of seeing those 'light bulb' moments as you teach students. For me, there is still a real excitement in learning new things and then being able to pass this knowledge on to others. As clinicians we have the privilege to touch the lives of thousands of patients over a career, but as a teacher and researcher that can be multiplied a hundred times over." (IS, senior academic)

Chapter 2 Securing a position

He manga wai koia kia kore e whitikia.

Is a river never to be crossed?

- What are tertiary institutions looking for?
- How can you position yourself to be considered for an academic position?
- What is a typical recruitment process for an early career academic?
- How do you apply for an early career academic position?
- What happens in a typical appointment process?
- Does everyone have an equal chance?

What are tertiary institutions looking for?

Despite romantic notions of academics sweeping through hallowed halls wearing their gowns in a Harry Potter-like scenario, academia today has a fairly consistent set of entry requirements and position expectations that are far more mundane—and a daily routine that often includes more bureaucracy than intellectual excitement.

A typical job advertisement for a new academic will ask for:

- appropriate qualifications—these could be both academic and professional
- relevant experience in the field—either as a practitioner or at the tertiary level
- evidence of researching, writing, presenting and publishing in the field
- knowledge of the disciplinary base for that field

- possible experience at tertiary level as a tutor, marker, lecturer or supervisor
- possible success in writing or winning research grants.

As an academic head or manager, I would also be interested in:
- personal qualities—self-motivation, commitment, perseverance, openness
- fit with the team—what experiences and skills complement or add to those of the existing team; will the applicant fit with our ways of working?
- appropriate cultural awareness or a willingness to learn
- willingness to contribute to the wider role of an academic—sitting on committees, mentoring others or engaging with the wider community.

An appointments committee will be made up of representatives who cover a range of institutional and departmental interests. Some of these interests are quite pragmatic; others are more strategic. They might have in mind the following questions:
- In what ways does the applicant contribute to diversity or equity goals of the institution?
- What potential does the candidate bring to enhancing the reputation of the institution through grants or awards?
- How will the applicant fare on research assessment exercises, such as PBRF?
- What evidence is there of knowledge of and commitment to the institution's vision or values, such as commitment to Te Tiriti o Waitangi?

How can you position yourself to be considered for an academic position?

A person doesn't wake up one morning and say to themselves, "I'm going to be an academic." It is usually a gradual realisation after completing a higher degree or engaging with a tertiary institution through research or practice. Several members of my Emerging Scholars Forum are experienced practitioners completing doctorates or on secondment from their permanent positions to undertake some tertiary level teaching or programme co-ordination. Their interest in moving into academia has evolved over time.

The first foray into academic life beyond your own study often comes when you are asked to undertake marking or become a teaching or research assistant. Some institutions call for expressions of interest from their students; in other institutions people just seem to be shoulder-tapped. In some disciplines, it is an expectation that masters students will mark essays or tutor undergraduates. In other disciplines, it seems to be a closed shop. When new academics ask me for advice on how to get noticed in order to secure a longer-term position when they are already in an institution, I offer several pieces of advice:

"It was a natural progression from my teaching. I was a drama teacher. I wanted to know why this happened and why that happened. That led me to do research. After my masters I went back into schools and that made me want even more to bridge the practice–theory divide. Teachers in classrooms are doing wonderful things that no one knows about. I wanted share what they did and apply theory to it." (CC, early career academic)

Get known

- Without being pushy, introduce yourself to those around you, attend meetings and seminars, eat your lunch in the common room and show an interest in others.

Offer to help out

- Put your hand up for marking or tutoring, join a committee or working party as a student representative, offer to give a guest lecture, take your turn to empty the dishwasher or engage in other collegial actions.

Establish your credibility

- Offer to hold a research seminar, get to know colleagues working in your field and gently let them know what you do in this area, make a copy of your publications available through the departmental bulletin board.

"Get to know people. Surprisingly basic, but at the same time there's a wide range of people to get to know—the subject-area librarian, other library staff, the support staff for your department, colleagues inside and outside the department, senior administrators and deans, research administrators, security guards, catering staff … anyone you see, really." (LG, early career academic)[4]

What is a typical recruitment process for an early career academic?

Recruitment and appointments processes vary markedly across institutions so it is hard to discuss a typical process or give a definitive timeline. In general, however, a head of department or programme leader identifies a gap that needs to be filled. They then consider the bigger picture. Have the needs of the department changed? Is it important to achieve a more diverse workforce? Does this area need new leadership? Is it better as a part-time position because of fluctuating enrolments?

A job description will be drawn up and a case prepared to begin the formal recruitment and appointments process. At this point, the academic manager might look around to see if this position could be filled by existing staff or someone on a short-term contract. If the position is small or short-term, it might follow a less formal process—and this is where being known might count in your favour. You will still need to provide a copy of your curriculum vitae (CV) and go through eligibility and verification checks but it might be a small introduction to the permanent appointment you are seeking. Several emerging scholars in my school have begun their careers as Graduate Teaching Assistants, Research Fellows or Lecturers on short-term contracts.

If the position is deemed to be significant or permanent, then it will follow a more formal process. The position will be advertised on the institution's website and possibly through recruitment agencies. There will be a more general advertisement accompanied by a full job description and details of someone to contact for more information.

Take the opportunity to find out more about the institution, faculty or programme. Use your networks. Ask academics you know about the institution and its expectations. Check out the institution's website. Get a feel for their vision, their values and their culture. If the institution's status matters to you, check out the various international ranking lists.

Get to know who works there. I was once asked in an interview who at that institution I admired and would want to work with. I was left scrambling for names—so it does help to get

"Prior to the interview I reviewed the university profiles to find out more about the academics on the interview panel. I arrived early and had a walk around the campus to get a sense of the place. I met with a friend who works there who explained about the university's new focus."
(CC, early career academic)

familiar with the place and who is there. If, finally, you think the job is for you, get your CV up to date and start putting together an application.

What is expected in an application for an early career academic position?

An application will generally include a covering letter, a completed application form, a CV (sometimes called a resumé), and names of confidential referees.

A covering letter highlights the particular position you are interested in and introduces who you are and where you are in your career now. It then briefly outlines why you consider yourself the right person for this position. It might also indicate your best contact details or periods of unavailability. Tailor your letter to match that position. Generic applications addressed to 'Dear Sir/Madam' at 'Your esteemed university' don't give a sense that you are genuinely interested in a position at that institution.

The next section will be an application form in which you detail how you meet the position criteria. If it is an electronic form, you have no choice but to complete the individual boxes in the order they are set out. If you are sending in a written application, you can tailor it to make it easy for the appointments committee to judge your qualities and experience against the position criteria. Don't make the committee go searching through pages of material to find important information. Here are my tips for making your application stand out:

- Read the job description thoroughly. Address the different expectations in your application. Use headings if you can, rather than big blocks of text. Use the language that they use without it appearing forced or insincere.
- Provide succinct and concrete evidence of your experience or aptitude to support your claims (dates, duration, roles undertaken or recognition given).
- Keep your language formal without being detached. Keep the committee's interest with sentences that get to the point rather than going off on tangents. Avoid over-enthusiasm or flattery.
- Proofread. Check the spelling of all important names. Get someone to read over your application and ask for critical feedback on content and style.

If you are attaching your CV, make sure it is up-to-date, organised with most recent information first (such as prior positions, qualifications or publications), neatly formatted, easy to follow and relevant—we don't really need to know about your school holiday job as a checkout operator or that you enjoy knitting—unless these details are making a significant point about your suitability for this position.

> *"Your CV gets you to an interview. The interview gets you the job. Tailor each step to fit the position you are applying for. Ask someone else to look at your application. It needs to stand out from the pack."* (KF, senior academic)

Finally, you will be asked to provide the names of confidential referees. Institutions prefer to have a confidential discussion with referees so that they can get a frank opinion of your suitability for the position. Written testimonials as part of your application or CV carry very little weight. Choose your referees carefully. Ask them ahead of time. Make sure that they know you and the key aspects of the position well enough to make useful comments about your suitability. Avoid possible conflicts of interest. Referees' comments will always remain confidential. Even if you later ask for feedback on the appointments process, you will be unable to access your referees' comments.

What happens in a typical appointment process?

You send your application in by the due date and wait. The applications will be collated and processed. If there are numerous applications they will be put through a filtering process to weed out those that don't meet the threshold for consideration. A committee might then review those that make the long list against the criteria for the position. The long list will be reduced to a short list. Those on the short list will be invited to an interview. There might also be an expectation that candidates complete a task such as presenting a research seminar, undertaking a socio-metric assessment or teaching a class. You will be given adequate time to prepare if that is the case.

The interview is the chance for you to build on what is in your application. Don't just answer the questions. Use the opportunity to engage with the panel. Use the 'state and expand' technique. By this I mean give a statement that answers the question and then expand with a concrete example:

Question: Have you conducted research in which you have had a leading role?

Possible answer: [State]. "Yes, first, when I undertook my PhD and, second, when I was the co-investigator on a university-school partnership project." [Expand]. "I learned different things about leading a project from each of these experiences. With my PhD, I had more responsibility for the decision-making but I had to learn from my mistakes as I went along. In the second piece of research, I was able to share these experiences and bounce ideas off my co-researcher as the research progressed. One example was …"

You might also be asked a behavioural interview question ("tell me about a time when …"), designed to get you to explain, with a real-life example, how you have acted in a particular situation. It helps to think of some of these ahead of time:

- Can you describe a time when you faced a challenge in your work? What was it and how did you deal with it?
- Can you describe a time when you successfully achieved a goal and outline for us what the key strategies were that led to your success?

The interview usually concludes with the interview chair asking if there is anything else you'd like to add. There might also be an opportunity for you to ask a question. Again, it helps to think of something ahead of time. For the 'anything to add' question, you might like to reiterate why you think you are a good fit for this position and the key attributes you bring. For the second question you might like to ask a fairly innocuous question about induction programmes or new initiatives the institution has in the pipeline. It is not the time to ask about salary. Ask about the salary range in your preliminary investigations on the position and bargain for your actual salary after you are offered the position and are at the stage of negotiating the terms and conditions.

"I was quite well-prepared. I had an idea of the types of questions that they might ask. I had mapped out what I would say in answer to questions like: 'Why are you applying for this job?'; 'Where do you see your research going in the future?'; or 'Tell us about your teaching philosophy.' I knew I would be quite nervous so I wanted to be well-rehearsed. A colleague told me to focus on three things I wanted to get across. That was good advice for me because I can get off track. My question for them at the end was to ask about room for growth and how I could contribute to course development." (CC, early career academic)

Does everyone have an equal chance?

It seems an appropriate place to talk about the lack of diversity in academic appointments in New Zealand. One example is that, despite gender equity policies, only 20% of full professors are women. If you are also of Māori or Pacific Island heritage, the journey to appointment, promotion and recognition is even harder. Academic institutions, wānanga aside, appear to be hardwired to do things as they have always been done and the glass ceilings are very real. For new academic staff it is important that you seek out willing mentors from amongst those who have made their way through the gender, sexuality, ableist or cultural roadblocks so that they can support you to do the same.

If any of my senior colleagues are reading this book, it is also important that you nurture the next generation of academics so we can have genuine diversity in the academic landscape.

"One thing I have noticed is the small number of Pasifika academics represented in higher education. These were my own observations as a Pasifika undergrad and postgrad student. However, now as a Pasifika lecturer it is about understanding the wider context of higher education and research. I am more aware of the underlying political tensions. Networking with other Pasifika academics has helped immensely, working collectively to make our presence known in the university." (JaM, early career academic)

Chapter 3 Developing your niche

Ahakoa he iti he pounamu

Although it is small, it is greenstone

- What can you expect before you start?
- What can you learn from reflecting on your career to date?
- How might you envision your academic future?
- How do you describe your area of expertise?
- How and when do you say yes or no to opportunities?
- How do you keep your focus?

What can you expect before you start?

Before you accept your position there are matters to consider. First, seek advice on the contract you are offered. Often new academics are so happy just to have a job that they agree without looking at the fine print. If the position has been offered to you, then they *really* want you. This is about the only time you have the upper hand. You can bargain (within reason) to have your salary more fairly recognise any prior professional experience, to build in a period of leave you were planning, to have the institution pay your relocation costs or to find a place for your child in their early childhood centre. Find out what is possible. You can also choose to have a superannuation plan carried over or to join the relevant union.

You accept the position and arrive full of nervous anticipation. Some institutions are very organised and have welcoming induction procedures—someone meets you, shows you around, unlocks your office and introduces you to key people. These institutions might also have a welcome pack outlining the important things you need to know, who to contact to answer your queries and a timeline for your induction programme. It is important that you take part in induction processes, orientations and professional development. It is a great way to meet people and get a feel for the organisation—and don't be afraid to ask questions. Go out of your way to introduce yourself to your leaders, managers and administrators so they can put a face to your name. If your institution has a pōwhiri for new staff or an introductory morning tea, take the opportunity to meet the people who will be your peers and possible support group.

Sadly, some institutions leave you to flounder—wandering around not sure who to ask. If your head of department is not around, your best bet is probably your departmental administrator. Eventually, the pieces of the puzzle fall into place, you are assigned a computer, a desk space, a teaching timetable and possibly a buddy. Enjoy this time getting to know your way around and meeting new people. You'll soon get a feel for how things operate and people will forgive your lapses while you are finding your feet.

> "*Everything is new:* Getting into the university or departmental culture as soon as possible is very important. Take walks around the campus—find out where the refreshment areas are and the library—spend time in the departmental tea room—go to lunch with people—talk—make connections—don't be afraid to make the first move." (University of Technology Sydney (UTS) website)[5]

If the department or centre does not provide you with a buddy or mentor, find someone who seems sympathetic and helpful to be your support person (see Chapter 5 for more on mentors).

The honeymoon period does not last for long and soon you will feel overwhelmed with information and expectations but pace yourself so you can manage all the competing demands (see Chapter 17).

> "*Advice I'd like to give:* No one expects you to teach, research or write like a veteran professor of 30 years. Be kind to yourself. Focus on you and do what you can realistically achieve in your first few years." (JT, early career academic)

When you are a little more settled, it is time to make some longer-term plans. One of the questions I remember my doctoral supervisor asking me was: "What do you want to be known for?" It was a similar question I faced when considering promotion to professor: "What are you a professor of?" My problem has been that not only am I an 'accidental academic', I have eclectic interests that make it hard for people—including promotions committees—to clearly see my central line of inquiry. To ensure new academics didn't face the same dilemma, one of the first sessions I planned for my Emerging Scholars Forum was "Developing your niche". What follows is a similar workshop I ran with a group of new academics at another institution to get them to think about what their niche might be. You might like to work your way through the activities individually or collectively.

"My research is diverse, sort of. I tend to work on vegetation dynamics, mainly the role of recruitment processes and how they affect local abundance, species coexistence, range limits, recovery after disturbance, invasions, restoration. I've tended to focus on herbaceous ecosystems. I've branched out into interesting related areas—the role of plant traits in predicting responses to perturbations, or the reversibility of ecosystem states, for instance—and it is this variety of general questions that continues to drive my curiosity. This is crucial. It means I might have forsaken answering one 'big' ecological question, but being a generalist means I still get really excited about plants every day of the week." (JM, mid-career academic)[6]

What can you learn from reflecting on your career to date?

Take to time to review what you have done prior to beginning your academic career. Here are some questions to help you focus.

Activity 1: Discuss the following questions
- What was the focus of your masters and/or doctorate?
- What else have you researched or written about?
- What key words do your provide for your articles?
- What subjects/topics do you teach?
- What area do you like to read about?
- What discipline or theory underpins your work?
- Whose work do you admire and what attracts you to their work?
- What is your passion?

"Locate yourself clearly in a disciplinary 'home' but remain open to links to other areas to enrich conceptual and research possibilities." (GM, early career academic)

How might you envision your academic future?

Note down the answers you have to the questions above then examine them more closely.

Activity 2: Review your answers to Activity 1
- What are the key words or topics that keep appearing?
- Are these the topics you want to be known for?
- Are there other achievements you are aiming for?
- Does the picture you are creating resonate with you?
- When someone asks you one day, "What are you a professor of?" what would you like to be able to say?

"You might need to carve out your own ideas and not follow the template. This can be a good thing. Cherish your unique contribution." (CC, early career academic)

How do you describe your area of expertise?

A useful activity is to have a brief statement that locates you in a field of research. Here is a strategy to get you started.

Activity 3: Make a concept map with the key words from Activity 2
- What are the ideas that link them all together?
- Try to put it into a short statement:
    I use (methodology/theory/approach) to (investigate/critique/explore) the (beliefs/stories/success) of (teachers/children/policy) in (schools/education/communities)…
- Ask yourself if this is closer to what you want to be known for.

"My research brings poststructuralist and feminist theories and methodologies to bear on a range of intersecting and overlapping interests in education that encompass architecture, gender, policy and practice, art, and music. Through the approaches of discourse analysis, genealogy, metaphor and narrative, and intersectionality, I aim to contribute to the renewal of the field of education studies in ways that highlight and promote the transformative power of education." (KL, early career academic)

How and when do you say yes or no to opportunities?

One of the most common questions I'm asked is when to say yes or no to opportunities that others present to you. Some new academics worry about offending the senior academics who make these offers or they worry that a similar opportunity might never present itself again. This activity was designed to help people reflect on prior dilemmas to prepare them for future choices they might face.

Activity 4: Remember times when you were invited to join research, writing, teaching or presentation opportunities.
Ask yourself these questions:
- Did the invitation fit with your vision of yourself?
- Did it resonate with your interests and strengths?
- Did it complement what you had already done or planned to do?
- Did it fit with your teaching or other research activities?

- Did it offer the chance to learn skills you need or network with people in areas of importance to you?
- Would it fit with your developing niche?

This will not be the only time you'll be invited to join a research project, write a book chapter or speak at a conference. Be strategic with your choices and be sensitive in your non-acceptance. At the same time, be open to something that might enhance your perspective or open your mind in ways you might not have imagined. That's one of the joys of academia—you never know what's coming next.

How do you keep your focus?

Your first academic position is an exciting time. There are many opportunities but there is also the work to be done that will pay your salary. Preparing for teaching, attending to departmental expectations and writing up your doctoral studies or prior research will keep you focused for the first few years.

As you find your feet you will start to make longer term plans (see Chapter 4). You will also be watching those around you and you might think that you have to achieve all the expectations in a short period of time. Becoming an academic is a career. It should take time. Your focus is to do the best for you and your students. Find a balance between focusing on where you want to be with taking relevant opportunities that come your way. Make sure that in your ambition to succeed you don't put too much pressure on yourself.

*"**Learn to say no.** Ah, the eternal truth of the time eater. I personally believe this is a small anteater type creature that sits under my desk and snuffles up time when I'm not looking. Learning to politely say 'no' to things that I don't have time to do on top of my teaching and research load is going to be one of my biggest challenges, because I'm an obliging sort of soul who likes taking advantage of opportunities. However, that's got to be balanced with a firm dose of reality. All the opportunities in the world aren't going to be any good if you're too overloaded to take advantage of any of them properly."* (LG, early career academic)

*"... **but know when to say yes.** Some opportunities will be golden. Learning how to discern which ones I should pick up and which ones I can safely say no to is going to be another key skill to develop. While I'm at it, I might try to sharpen my mindreading and fortune telling skills as well"* (LG, early career academic)

Chapter 4 Planning your career pathway

Māu anō e rapu he oranga

Your livelihood is in your own hands

- What is your ultimate goal?
- What are some useful considerations along the way?
- What other responsibilities might make calls on your time?
- What other opportunities might present themselves?
- What is important in the end?

I was quite taken aback recently when a young colleague said, "But you don't know how competitive it is out there nowadays." I stopped to think about when becoming an academic become a competition. When did being an academic lose a sense of achievement in itself and become a race to some unknown endpoint? Is this what the neoliberal university has become—a place where young academics feel a sense of failure when they have barely begun? Let's put this all into perspective.

"The biggest problem I faced: Operating within such a competitive neoliberal 'accountability' type environment." (JT, early career academic)

What is your ultimate goal?

We each come to academic life for different reasons and via different, often serendipitous, pathways. For some, the career plan is simple—doctoral candidate, post-doctoral researcher, junior academic and on through the ranks to full professor. For others, there are detours into management positions or for whom a management position is the ultimate goal. Yet others become so immersed in their subject that the gathering and dissemination of new knowledge is reward enough. A good place to start is to look around and see who you admire. By reading their webpages or chatting to them in person, you can see how their career has developed and what decisions and milestones they reached along the way.

Which of the three main aspects of academia—teaching, research or service—interests you most? What are the achievements you wish to achieve in each field?

"Remember the real goal in research, teaching and service is not your own career but in making a real difference through the work that you do."
(PO, senior academic)

What are some useful considerations along the way?

Within academia there are people for whom teaching is a rewarding and fulfilling activity. They get pleasure from watching students develop an understanding and even a passion for their subject area. They enjoy the performance of a large lecture situation, the intensity of postgraduate supervision or the 'aha' moments in a practical workshop. Some of these academics are recognised at their departmental, faculty, or institutional level and a few of these go on to win national awards.

As an emerging academic, taking opportunities offered to you in different teaching formats and with different lecturers is a good way to expand your repertoire and find what works for you. It is always important to note down the different activities you try and the contribution you make to course development, implementation and evaluation. In this way you are gathering evidence that will be useful in appraisal, continuation, promotion and award nomination situations. (It will also be helpful when research assessment exercises, such as when the PBRF (Performance-Based Research Fund)[7] 6-yearly rounds are undertaken.

Similarly with service, note what those you admire have contributed over their careers towards departmental, faculty, university, discipline and community fields. While meetings can seem tedious to some, it is part of your role to contribute to policy and decision-making at a range of levels—it is also part of your workload expectation. Rather than making meetings and committees a chore, gain a working knowledge of your institution's structure and where your skills or interests might best fit. See it as a positive contribution and you'll be surprised how you come to understand what appeared at first to be mystifying complexities. Eventually, you might see how, in your small way, you can make a difference to aspects of institutional life.

Finally, you are developing a research career. In the sciences, this is often mapped out as you join a research centre or work alongside an academic with a strong profile. For those in the humanities, this is often a more solitary journey, where there are not teams of people to support you or large grants to fund your research direction.

Your institution will outline quantifiable expectations for you to reach, such as numbers of peer reviewed publications or total funds received in grants. Your institution might also want indications of quality such as course reviews or recognition by your peers. Make yourself familiar with these expectations and map out your goals over the next 5 to 10 years as in the example below (taken from the teacher education field).

	Yr 1 goal setting	Yr 2	Yr 3	Yr 4	Yr 5	Longer
Teaching	Tutoring					
	Teaching		Course leader		New course development	
	Supervision	2 Masters	2 Doctoral			
	Clinical/practicum				Liaison role	
Service	School	School Research Committee				
	Faculty		Undergraduate degree working party		Faculty Research Committee	
	Discipline/Assn	Attend NZARE	Attend AERA	Review for NZJES	Conference committee	Editorial board
Research	2 articles		Complete book from doctorate			
	1 book chapter					Marsden
	1 in-house grant			Faculty grant		Fast Start

Continuation — PBRF — Research & study leave — Promotion to SL

What other responsibilities might make calls on your time?

Remember your career is only one facet of your life. A colleague with two young children spoke of how he felt the pressure to say yes to everything he was offered or his career would be put at risk. I suggested that he would be working on his career for the rest of his life and that everyone would have different circumstances that might speed up or slow down their career progression. I added that it was not a race. What was the point of matching himself against colleagues who did not have family or community commitments? I suggested he slow down and enjoy the ride—spend more time with his family. He had his whole career to achieve his goals. When he paused to think about this, he said he felt that a weight was lifted off his shoulders.

> *"Two things: The first is keeping my family as a priority which has meant that I have continued to enjoy my job without being resentful towards it. The second has been staying engaged with community activities—the ivory tower can be an isolating place and it is important to stay connected your communities of interest."* (JM, early career academic)

Many other opportunities and responsibilities will come along. Each one could enrich you as a person and add in some way to your career. Examine them for the advantages they offer—a different perspective, an insight into a better practical understanding. I if nothing else you might have interesting stories to tell in your lectures.

I have taken several breaks over my career. After being in teacher education for some time I travelled overseas with my family and found myself supply teaching in London schools before I secured an academic position. Not only did it test my skills as a teacher, it gave me opportunities to practice many of the theories I had been espousing in undergraduate lectures back in New Zealand. Later in my career, I had 3 years as a policy advisor in Wellington. This time I saw policy making from the inside—invaluable experiences that greatly enriched my teaching and writing when I returned to academia.

While taking time off to be with family, to travel, to take up a visiting academic position or to return to your professional field might not add to a speedy career progression, these opportunities make you a more grounded and interesting academic when you return.

> *"The most enjoyable thing I did: I found a wonderful colleague who reminded me to balance my professional pursuits with life outside academia."* (JT, early career academic)

What other opportunities might present themselves?

One of the things that I remember about my early career and that I see in my younger counterparts is knowing when to say 'yes' and when to say 'no' (see also Chapter 3). As an emerging academic you are so flattered to be asked to join a research project or contribute a chapter to an edited collection that you jump at the chance.

The lesson I learned along the way was that many such opportunities will present themselves. Rather than finding yourself overwhelmed or going down a research path that doesn't fit your interests, take time to consider how the opportunity fits your developing portfolio. I'm not saying turn down everything that doesn't immediately appeal—some of these opportunities might be life changing or might take you down an amazingly rich and worthwhile path. My advice is:

- Consider the opportunity.
- Does it relate in some way to your interest, skills and developing niche?
- Will it strengthen some aspect of your academic life or portfolio?
- Ask for clear expectations of results, support, timeframes and recompense before agreeing.

There are ways you can ask for more detail without sounding pushy—and ways to say 'no' that keep the relationship intact.

> *"Learn to say no, at least to some things. When you first start up, you feel like you have to impress your workplace, so you tend to end up saying 'yes' to everything. Either that, or like me, you didn't realise you could say 'no'. While busy people make time to do all the tasks they take on, in academia this actually comes at a cost. By agreeing to every committee you're asked to sit on, and doing all the admin jobs around the department, as well as lots of teaching, you actually cut into your quality time to do research, and to hang around with those who [help with] your research (your Post-Grads). It is good to be busy, but not at the expense of the most important task on your Job Description. I have been poor at saying no and now have learnt to say 'I'll get back to you on that' or 'I need to check my diary first'. I still say 'yes' way too often. Saying no shouldn't be a reflection that you're not a 'team-player' but rather, you are trying to get a good balance between research, teaching and admin."* (JM, mid-career academic)

What is important in the end?

I see new academics who set themselves impossible goals. They feel that they have to make their mark in a very short space of time or they will be left behind. I know I have said it before but academia is a way of life. You have a lifetime, or a large part of it, to achieve your goals. Don't try to rush your career achievements so quickly that you become obsessively self-focused and cease to enjoy what an academic career offers. What matters in the end is that you have done a job that gives you intrinsic as well as extrinsic rewards.

> *"Best advice I received:* You only need to do 'enough' … you are already doing enough! As an emerging scholar I felt that I was expected to do a superhuman amount of work, to keep doing more and achieving in all areas. I was really grateful when colleagues advised me to be clear on what it was that I actually needed to do to fulfil the requirements of my job and to not try and do everything else I was being asked to do, or felt that I should be doing. I was glad for help with setting priorities and working out realistic plans." (MM, early career academic)

In the following interview extract, an experienced academic puts his career in perspective:

> *"I'm a late academic.* In a formal sense I came to the university late in life but I taught, researched and gave service to my discipline long before I became an academic. Coming to the university wasn't that much different to the life I led before but it was about leaving a legacy. What did I want to do with the rest of my life? What did I learn about being a theatre maker in the community that I could pass on? The great joy about coming to the university was that I realised that I had so much to learn. I knew a lot but only about a narrow area. The best piece of advice I can give is to take advantage of all the opportunities—seminars, lectures, every accidental corridor conversation. Don't sit in your office or at home—come and be part of the communal life of the university. I think if you come later in life to an academic position you value what academia offers more than someone who has known little else. I think my other piece of advice, and this comes from having done lots of other jobs, is to recognise that being in a university is a gilded life. It comes with enormous privileges—the lives we lead, the money we make, the travel we do, the intelligent conversations we are able to have—we are not going down mines or struggling every day to pay the mortgage. Do things that feed your soul not just tick boxes. Do things that matter, not just count." (PO, senior academic)

Chapter 5 Finding a mentor

Whāia te māramatanga

Seek enlightenment

- What is a mentor?
- Are there different kinds of mentors?
- How do you find a mentor?
- Should you participate in a formal mentoring programme?
- What might you expect from a mentor?

What is a mentor?

When I think of a mentor, I think of someone whose career is far enough ahead to be able to offer wise advice, open doors and be a sounding board—but not so far ahead that they have forgotten how hard it was to get there. The relationship between a mentor and their mentee is based on mutual trust and respect. The relationship might take some time to establish.

> *"Find good mentoring. It does not simply happen, even if there are faculty structures in place. It is about relationships, meeting people and establishing who those people are that you esteem and value their advice."*
> (JM, early career academic)

In some fields, such as many of the science disciplines, your introduction to academia is more of an apprenticeship. You often join a cohort of students who go through together and gain experiences that prepare you for academic life as part of a research team or centre. You often have one or more senior academics who take on a mentoring role. In other disciplines, this is not so clear-cut.

I prefer to participate (both as a mentor or mentee) in a mentoring relationship that is not tied to formal procedures such as performance appraisal or professional development. The literature in this field discriminates between formal mentoring, which is more functional and job-related (often called coaching) and informal mentoring, which is more relational, whole-of-career focused, and fluid. One mentoring site defines the characteristics of the two roles this way:

Coaching characteristics:	Mentoring characteristics:
• Managers coach all of their staff as a required part of the job • Coaching takes place within the confines of a formal manager–employee relationship • Focuses on developing individuals within their current jobs • Interest is functional, arising out of the need to ensure that individuals can perform the tasks required to the best of their abilities • Relationship tends to be initiated and driven by an individual's manager • Relationship is finite—ends as an individual transfers to another job	• Takes place outside of a line manager–employee relationship, at the mutual consent of a mentor and the person being mentored • Is career-focused or focuses on professional development that may be outside a mentee's area of work • Relationship is personal—a mentor provides both professional and personal support • Relationship may be initiated by a mentor or created through a match initiated by the organization • Relationship crosses job boundaries • Relationship may last for a specific period of time in a formal program, at which point the pair may continue in an informal mentoring relationship

Source: http://www.management-mentors.com/resources/corporate-mentoring-programs-resources-faqs

Are there different kinds of mentors?

You may find that your institution has a formal mentoring programme and you are assigned a mentor or you may find yourself wandering in an academic wilderness trying to find someone who might help you with your career planning.

> *"Get a mentor. Whether official or unofficial, having someone to talk stuff over with and ask for advice is going to be vital."*
> (LG, early career academic)

My institution recommends that all staff might benefit from mentors at different times in their career, not just as new appointments. Suggestions include:

- a teaching mentor to improve your teaching skill or develop a new teaching approach
- a research mentor, especially if your assigned mentor is not in your disciplinary area

- a recently confirmed or promoted staff member to assist you with your applications
- an experienced supervisor to mentor you through your first supervisions.

As with the purpose of the mentoring relationship, the process might vary markedly. You might be looking for someone to give you career advice which you then act on by yourself. You might be looking for someone who walks alongside your career for a longer period of time and who will see you through the ups and downs. You might be looking for someone who is really just a sounding board for your ideas. You might be looking for someone with status who can open doors and act as a sponsor for you. You might have more than one person because they are each fulfilling a different need. These relationships might vary in length and intensity. The best advice is to find what works for you with the understanding that this will change over time.

I recently attended a professional development session on mentoring and sponsoring. I hadn't met the idea of academic sponsoring before. My understanding now is that it is going further than coaching or mentoring. A coach would help you plan your next career moves; a mentor would provide a range of suggestions to meet these goals; a sponsor would put your name forward for particular opportunities. It made me think how and when I might sponsor a mentee. If you are a mentor, you might like to find out more about academic sponsoring. If you are a mentee, you might like to raise this idea with your mentor. You will, of course, need to be subtle about how you approach this, as it is your mentor's right to decide when they act as a sponsor or advocate. Their reputation could suffer if they make a poor recommendation.

A sponsoring relationship takes longer to evolve as mutual trust and respect is built up between the partners. It did make me think, however, about having a discussion with my senior colleagues about when and how we might be a coach, a mentor or a sponsor. Here are some examples I could use:

	Coaching	Mentoring	Sponsoring
Teaching	• Discuss teaching achievements and future plans	• Focus on more strategic opportunities for developing teaching style and content	• Suggest to a colleague that the mentee could teach into their course • Put mentee forward for a teaching award
Research	• Review publication and presentation achievements	• Focus on strategic publication outlets • Suggest funding opportunities	• Co-publish with mentee • Co-edit a special issue or edited book with mentee • Include mentee in research funding proposals
Service	• Discuss the mentee's goals and how they fit with the institutional leadership framework	• Encourage mentee to widen focus from departmental to faculty or institutional service • Suggest mentee considers editorial board or conference committee membership	• Nominate mentee for important committees or to fill a vacancy • Put mentee's name forward for reviewing, editorial boards or discipline association roles

*"**Team up with a senior academic.** Life is pretty lonely in academia sometimes. You feel time-pressured, pulled from all sides, developing subjects with little help, and worry that your research is not going as well as it could. Indeed, you might even feel career success competition from other academics. I felt this way too, mainly because my University didn't really have a mentor programme in place to guide me through the complexity of academic life. So, for many years, I just put up with this. I assumed that you just got on with things. It wasn't till I teamed up with a senior academic (from another university), in what really was a chance interaction, that I started to get some mentoring that helped me figure out 'my job'. This mentoring, unofficial as it was, made a huge difference to how I felt about my place. How to think about priorities, how to see my role in academia, and how to interact in my research field—none of this was ever made explicit."* (JM, mid-career academic)

How do you find a mentor?

If you haven't been assigned one or found one along the way then it might take some time and effort. Good mentoring requires relationship building. The two parties need to find a point of connection through location, discipline, topic or perhaps methodology. Is there someone who has caught your eye? You might know of them through their teaching, research or writing. They might have a reputation for assisting younger colleagues or providing opportunities. It is hard to start a relationship from scratch. Many senior academics mentor those they have supervised, taught or researched with. If you haven't found a mentor this way then I suggest you consider:

- What are you looking for in a mentor?
- What expectations do you have for the relationship?
- Ask around your colleagues, including the person who does your appraisal.
- Consider who might be a good fit for your needs and interests.
- Arrange to meet this person and outline your request without sounding pushy.
- Allow the person time to think it over, read some of your work or ask around about you.
- Be prepared for them to say no—there might be many reasons why this is not going to work for them.
- If it doesn't work out, be gracious and thank them for their time. You may ask for other suggestions.
- If it does work out, negotiate how it might work for both of you.
- Mentorship doesn't have to be a monogamous relationship—you might have several contacts that you meet to discuss different aspects of your work or career with.

Should you participate in a formal mentoring programme?

My advice is to give it a go. Some people prefer to find someone who fits their personality or working style rather than be given someone they don't connect with. If your nominated mentor isn't working for you, there might still be useful things to be gained from the formal programme—career guidance, visiting speakers, networking opportunities or useful resources. I always find I can take something away from professional development seminars, whether it is a good idea, a new perspective, an understanding of what it's like for others or an insight into how the system works.

What might you expect from a mentor?

There are two parts to the answer to this question—what might you expect and what might they expect from you. Here are my suggestions:

What might you expect?	What might they expect?
• someone who is genuinely interested in your personal journey or at least a part of it	• someone who respects them and values what they have to say
• someone who has the knowledge, experience or skills you need at that time	• someone who sets and keeps appointments
• someone who is clear about what they can and can't offer so the relationship has definite boundaries	• someone who is able to articulate their goals and be willing to work within realistic timelines
	• someone who is open and honest about their strengths and weaknesses
• someone who is willing to listen and understand things from an early career perspective	• someone who is willing to listen and try some of their mentor's suggestions
• someone who offers sound advice but allows you to weigh it up as well	• someone who doesn't overstep the boundaries of the relationship (that is, is not constantly needy or overly demanding)
• someone who has the time and energy to put into the relationship	• someone who is not defensive about the advice they are given
• someone who knows when it is time for both of you to move on.	• someone who leaves the relationship with acceptance and gratitude.

Finding a mentor was one of the most common pieces of advice given to me when I talked to colleagues about this book. Find one that works for you and make the best of it. Use your mentor's time wisely and strategically. Don't worry if you need to expand your circle of mentors and don't feel bad if the relationship runs its course. Exit with grace, as you never know when your paths will cross again.

"Advice I'd like to give: the importance of 'managing up"—i.e., knowing what to ask your supervisors and mentors to do." (JW, senior academic)

Chapter 6 Becoming a tutor or teaching assistant

Ma whero ma pango ka oti ai te mahi

With red and black together the work will be complete

- Why undertake tutoring?
- How do you make tutorials worthwhile?
- How might you structure your tutorials?
- What is your role in preparing students for assignments and examinations?
- What is your role in marking assignments and examinations?
- How do you prepare a teaching portfolio?

Why undertake tutoring?

In some institutions, such as polytechnics, a tutor is a formal position that has a specific job description, role expectations, and career progression. In other institutions, it is a looser term that it is used to describe early career teaching opportunities, such as taking tutorials. The role might also be called a 'teaching or graduate teaching assistant' (TA or GTA). It is the looser tutor role I am referring to in this chapter.

Finding yourself thrust into a room with an unknown group of uninspired undergraduates can be daunting. But tutoring offers many opportunities. First, when you sit in on the accompanying lectures you start to engage with the material in a different way. You are constantly thinking about how you will enable students to unpack the content that has been presented. Second, you begin to repackage the material in ways that will help students see its relevance to the overall themes and concepts of the course. Third, you get introduced to ideas and readings that enhance your own understanding of the subject matter.

How do you make tutorials worthwhile?

I'm sure you remember trudging off to a tutorial taken by a nervous postgraduate student who barely knew the material and struggled to answer your questions. If you are passionate about the subject matter, here is your chance to inspire the next generation of scholars. In many large undergraduate courses, tutorial discussion material or readings may be assigned but there might also be times when you are left to your own devices so you have a chance to approach the material creatively.

> *"Planning is the best antidote for the nerves that many people feel when teaching a subject for the first time or meeting a new group of students. It is also the only way to ensure that your educational objectives are achieved. Planning begins with thinking about how you would like your students to approach their learning in your subject and what you would like them to understand, know or be able to do by the end of the semester."*
> (UTS website)

I think there are three elements to being a successful tutor: preparation, engagement and sense making.

1. Preparation

- Read the course syllabus. Be familiar with the course objectives, themes, and key concepts. Have a sense of where this course fits into the bigger picture of the discipline. Is it to introduce students to key concepts and methods or does it assume key understandings and move students to a higher level of complexity?
- Read the text or set readings far enough ahead of time for the accompanying lectures to make sense as you listen in. If there is anything you are not sure about ask other tutors, a course lecturer or the co-ordinator.
- Attend the lecture, listen to the podcast or watch the video recording (if available). Take notes on key ideas, examples of these ideas, and links to the readings or other things that will help with your tutorial.
- You might find a graphic organiser helps you connect the key themes and concepts.

- Sit in on tutorials in another course to help you get a sense of how much can be covered in the time allocated and to see how more experienced tutors approach the material.
- Plan out how you might allocate the time in the tutorial (see later section in this chapter).

2. Engagement

One of the good features of a tutorial is that the numbers are smaller than in a lecture situation and you have the opportunity to build a relationship with your students. In fact, you carry an important responsibility as the human face of the course. Not many lecturers will know all of their students' names but as a tutor you will. When you have your first tutorial, take time to introduce yourself—what you've been studying, why you are passionate about your area, what you bring to your role as a tutor. Get to know your students a little, learn some names, and set a tone for positive interaction. Explain how you would like the tutorials to operate and what your expectations are (for example, turn off cell phones, show courtesy by listening to others and respond in a collegial manner).

"Teaching in tutorials provides more scope for learner involvement and participation. The range of tasks and activities one can set a small group is limited only by the imagination of the teacher. There are many advantages of small group participatory learning. Interaction among students helps to build group cohesion and enhances their capacity to work in a collaborative way. Group work recognises that learning is an active rather than purely passive process. There is an opportunity for you to listen, to tap the knowledge and experience of students, and for them to share and test their ideas and interpretations." (UTS website)

Find ways to get your students to engage and contribute. Your tutorials need some structure and activities to get students talking. Asking vague questions like: 'What was the lecture about? or 'What is the author saying in the article?' will only elicit blank looks. Here are some of examples of more engaging activities:

- **Non-assessed quiz.** From the readings or the lecture, design a quick quiz. Students earn a point per correct answer and a bonus point if they explain why the answer

"You may need to rearrange the furniture. This is a very important factor in tutorials. Providing a pleasant physical environment will create a more intimate atmosphere. Try arranging furniture in a semi circle with you as the focus at the start or in clusters for group work. Avoid seating students in straight rows if you want them to discuss ideas or work together." (UTS website)

is correct. (I still find chocolate fish are great motivators.) You can assign students (or ask for volunteers) to prepare future quizzes.
- **Pair interviews.** In pairs, the students take turns interviewing each other about the readings or lecture. You can provide the questions or they can invent their own.
- **Think, pair, share.** (1) <u>Think:</u> Students are given a minute to jot down their answer to a question. (2) <u>Pair:</u> They share their answer with one other person. Between them they compile the best answer. (3) <u>Share:</u> They can either share with another pair or with the class. This is a good activity for students who find speaking in front of others intimidating.
- **Concept matching.** You prepare a sheet with concepts or terms down one side, then definitions down the other. You can use this in different ways. You could leave one or other side blank and get the students in pairs or small groups to complete the missing answers or you could cut up the completed sheet and get them to match the concept with its definition.
- **Concept web.** The cut up concepts (from the activity above) are provided to the students in small groups. They are asked to arrange them in an interesting way that they can later share with the whole class. They might put them in clusters of like ideas, a timeline, Venn diagram or join them with lines to make a web. The discussion this generates is more important than the shape they create. It gives you an opportunity to gauge their level of understanding.

"Spending too much time on preparing sessions and including too much content in these sessions are common pitfalls for some new academic staff. A gulf can develop between what is being taught and what is being learned by students. Keep your sessions simple. Concentrate on teaching a number (3–5) of main points effectively." (UTS website)

3. Sense making

While the ideas suggested above can generate discussion and engagement, in the end your role is to help the students make sense of the course content. The following questions are designed to help you think about what you want students to work towards over the course of your tutorials:

- Do students have a sense of the wider field or discipline within which this course sits?
- Do students understand a little of the history and development of the field?
- Are students gaining an understanding of the key ideas, concepts, theories and terms used in this field?
- Are students gaining an understanding of who the key theorists and writers are in this field?
- Are students gaining an understanding of key debates and issues in this field?
- Can students see why they are learning this material?
- Can students see the relevance of the readings and lecture notes to the bigger ideas in the field?
- Are students developing the skills needed to process the course material or undertake the related practical tasks?
- Can students see how the assignments are designed to help them show their understanding or apply key ideas?

How might you structure your tutorials?

Your tutorial might vary from a 1-hour lecture follow-up to a clinical workshop or lab lasting several hours. Plan to break the time allocated into useful and logical sections. Here is a suggested format:

- **Introduction** (outlining what you are going to cover)
- **Review** (finding out what students gained from the lecture and what questions they have)
- **Processing** (helping students to unpack the content, the readings and/or the key ideas)
- **Conclusion** (returning to key points; providing signposts for the next lecture's content and readings).

"Practical classes can provide opportunities for students to begin to experience what it is like to be a professional in their discipline area—to work on a practical problem, communicate solutions and give and receive constructive criticism. Practical sessions by definition require student involvement. They vary widely between disciplines but some of the common aims can include: encouraging enquiry and exploration; linking theory to practice; [and] teaching practical skills." (UTS website)

Here is the format broken into chunks of time for a 1-hour session:

Arrive ahead of time to check room • layout • lighting • IT (computer, digital projector and screen) • whiteboard and pens • practical materials or resources	5–10 minutes (if room is not being used beforehand)
Introduction and housekeeping • welcome, reminders, notices • taking roll (if expected) • assignment preparation or debriefing	5–10 minutes
Review • relating back to previous lecture • checking students understand the key points from this lecture • explaining any terminology or examples that they are unsure of • discussing the relevance, significance or application of what was covered	10 minutes
Processing • See the suggestions in the earlier sections in this chapter.	30 minutes
Conclusion • how this week's lecture links to next week • what to look for in next week's readings or notes	5 minutes
Available (for individual questions or assistance) • in classroom or move to your office	5–10 minutes
	60+ minutes

What is your role in preparing students for assignments and examinations?

There are two main ways you will be involved with assignments and examinations as a tutor: (1) providing students with advice on how to approach the tasks or questions (see Chapter 7 for extra ideas); and (2) marking in-class, online and hardcopy assignments and examination papers.

Here are my thoughts on some useful advice you can give your students when approaching essays. You can adjust these questions to suit different types of assignments.

- **Answer the question**
  - What is the question asking you to do—discuss, analyse, compare, contrast …?
  - What do these verbs mean?
  - What hints does the question give you—for example, timeframe, context, readings or theorists?
  - What does the question indicate should be included in or excluded from the answer?
- **Construct an argument** (Get students to complete these sentence starters to shape their essay)
  - I will argue that …
  - I will support this argument by discussing …
  - I will begin by reviewing the literature on …
  - I will provide examples by …
  - I will support the argument with evidence by citing …
- **Plan the essay to fit the word limit**

When I'm working on a piece of writing, I start with the suggested word length, and then divide the piece into suitably sized sections. I make sure that I include all the expected elements, such as introduction, literature, definition of terms, main body of the argument and conclusion. I then estimate how many words each section will need. This is helpful to make sure I attend to the important aspects and don't waste time on irrelevant points. It also means I am not daunted by the size of the task as I frame it as a series of smaller linked sections. I then allocate blocks of time to deal with each section. I also include time to review and revise what I've written. Here is an example:

1. Introduction (250 words)	2. Literature review (300 words)	3. Outline of the three examples (250 words)	4. Example 1 (500 words)
5. Example 2 (500 words)	6. Example 3 (500 words)	7. Conclusion and implications (200 words)	Total (2500 words)

- Write the essay/assignment
    - Write each section
    - Make smooth links between the sections
    - Review the logic and check you've answered the question
    - Return to the beginning to be sure what you said you would do, is what you did
    - Proofread and revise
    - Give to a critical friend
    - Check references and referencing convention
    - Read, revise, proofread (again) and hand in on time.

What is your role in marking assignments and examinations?

Part of your role as a tutor will involve marking assignments and examinations. Assignment and examination grades are high stakes. It is important that your marking is as fair and rigorous as possible yet done within a reasonable time frame. As a new marker you can be anxious about whether your judgement is correct—have you been too hard or too lenient? Here are some suggestions to help you:

- Find out about the departmental guidelines, marking protocols and expectations.
- You can ask if someone could show you exemplars or if they could to check mark samples of your marking and discuss how well you have done this.
- If there is a marking rubric, this can help clarify expectations; if not you could consider creating one based on the assignment criteria (check this with the course co-ordinator). A rubric helps you with your judgement making. Students also find them helpful. I give these out when the assignments are first explained so students can use them as a planning guide.
- Find out if this is a formative or summative assignment. If it is a formative one, providing students with feedback on how they could improve is appreciated. A summative assignment, such as an examination, is assessing what they have learned overall and often doesn't require feedback. I write my initial comments in pencil if I'm

marking hard copies so that I can remove any comments at a later stage if I change my mind as their essay unfolds (it's easier to do this when marking online). When you give a summary statement try to be specific about what was done well and what could improve.
- Many course co-ordinators organise check-marking or moderation to ensure consistency across markers. This is a useful activity for you to engage in to improve your judgement-making.
- When I have finished, I find it helpful to put my assignments into order according to the grades as a final check—Was this one really better than that one? Were these two as good as each other?
- It is important to keep accurate records—making sure that the correct student name and ID are recorded against the correct grade. Mistakes can be undone but they can cause student anxiety and administrative headaches.

How do you prepare a teaching portfolio?

When I began lecturing, tertiary teaching was not discussed as a skill to be learned and honed. I think you were expected to pick up good teaching by osmosis. Most new academics began by modelling themselves on lecturers they had been taught by or colleagues they admired. Becoming a supervisor was the same—except that you had fewer role models to draw on. Today, tertiary teaching is a field with its own qualifications, conferences and journals. As a lecturer you will be expected to document your teaching experiences and articulate your philosophy of teaching. Start recording your ideas and experiences now.

As a tutor or graduate teaching assistant aiming for an academic position, you will be expected to be developing your teaching philosophy. In this you could outline what kind of a teacher you wish to be, where your influences have come from and what kind of learning environment you wish to set up for your students. I suggest you record:

- The details of the courses you have been involved in (name, level, role)
- Tasks you were responsible for (taking tutorials, marking assignments or examinations)
- Innovations you implemented (online discussion group, peer assessment)

- Feedback or evaluation comments (from students, colleagues or external observers)
- Adjustments you made to your teaching as a result of feedback
- Experience as a supervisor or mentor
- Professional development you have undertaken.

From here, you can take time to think about the nature of teaching, and how the kind of a teacher you wish to be impacts on your teaching as a professional practice. You might find it helpful to attend a tertiary teaching course, read about the scholarship of teaching and learning (SoTL) or talk to colleagues who have won teaching awards in your faculty. You can also access exemplary portfolios from your teaching and learning centre or Ako Aotearoa, the National Tertiary Teaching Centre.

> "If I visualise my journey as a teacher it looks a bit like a braided river: wandering in its bed but always coming back to the main stream eventually." (mid-career academic, Ako Aotearoa)[8]

Try to write a succinct paragraph that encapsulates your teaching philosophy. Some people find it helpful to use a metaphor or visual motif to express the essence of their beliefs about the links between teaching and learning.

You might also like to collect examples of your course planning, handouts, activities or assignment formats. You can include photos of your classes or activities but be sure to ask those who appear in your photographs if you can have their permission to use these in your portfolio.

> "I also created a booklet containing photos, lesson planning and student feedback (all with the consent of students) to act as a teaching portfolio of my recent work." (CC, early career academic)

Chapter 7 Developing your teaching

Naku te rourou nau te rourou ka ora ai te iwi

With your basket and my basket the people will live well

- How do you gain teaching experience?
- What do you need to know about undergraduate teaching?
- How do you incorporate skill development?
- What do you need to know about postgraduate teaching?
- What is culturally responsive teaching?
- How might you teach in more innovative formats?

How do you gain teaching experience?

I remember my first tertiary class quite clearly. I was lecturing to a class of third year teacher education students about the teaching of language to primary students. I introduced myself and wrote across the board in large letters, "What is language?" I wanted to start my class with a lively discussion about the importance of language and communication. I waited expectantly. There was a long silence. Eventually one bright spark called out, "We don't know. That's what you are here to tell us!" I learned an important lesson. Even to this day, I take time to make a connection with the class. I try to find out a little more about them. What point are they at in their programme? What have they covered already? I ask other lecturers about the group. I spend time on the first day telling them a little about myself, what I teach and research and what I'm looking forward to as I teach this course. Today, you can do much of that electronically before a course commences. You can also ask them to tell you a little about themselves before you meet.

If you are already employed as a tutor or graduate teaching assistant opportunities to contribute to lectures will usually come your way. Take these and use them as a chance to develop your style. Try out approaches and activities you have seen other lecturers use. Find what works for you. Ask the lecturer or other tutors sitting in the lecture for feedback. Could you be heard? Were you clear? Did you pace yourself well? Did you engage the audience? What could you do better?

In one of our large undergraduate courses we have short 10-minute "spotlight sessions." Here we ask our postgraduate students to talk briefly on an aspect of their research topic that fits with the content of the course. It is a great way to get experience without it being too daunting. You could suggest this idea to your course co-ordinator or departmental teaching and learning committee.

The move from tutoring to teaching means that you will gain a greater understanding of how courses are put together and where they fit in a programme. It is helpful to find out how courses are developed—what are the guidelines for titles, course descriptions, learning outcomes and assessment tasks? Why do some courses have examinations and others not? What do the alpha-numerics mean? Is this course part of a suite of courses or a professional programme? What is the graduate profile for the programme? If it is a professional programme, how do the courses you teach contribute to professional accreditation?

"As a new lecturer, it was really important for me to understand how the course I was about to teach situates within the wider programme. I wanted to know the history of the course and how this course followed on from previous courses. When I learned the history of the course and the passion of the lecturers advocating an indigenous world view, I felt committed to the course and its intentions and purpose." (JaM, early career academic)

What do you need to know about undergraduate teaching?

Most, but not all, undergraduate teaching, especially first year level, is in large lecture theatres. If I am in a large lecture situation, I find that my teaching is more of a performance. Not that I am any less authentic but I need to work harder to engage and keep students' attention. I project my voice, move across the lecture theatre floor to address the students from different angles and use gesture for emphasis. I am more structured in my lecture format and I keep the pace moving to maintain interest and motivation. I build in 'micro breaks' where students can jot down a reflection or discuss a question with the person beside them. I provide skeleton lecture notes electronically ahead of time to give students an idea of the lecture direction. At the lecture, I flesh these out on PowerPoint or verbally with examples or relevant anecdotes. That way, students still need to come to lectures to get a full understanding of the course content.

I start my lecture by briefly reminding the students of the key ideas of the course and how today's lecture fits with those, including relating it to what we covered last time. I usually structure the lecture around some key questions that I will address during the lecture and at the end sum up the relevance of what we have just explored. I relate the content to the set text or recommended readings to pique their interest so they will read these more thoroughly and use them to extend their understanding.

One mistake new lecturers often make is that they over-rely on PowerPoint. They think they are going to forget what to say so they fill their slides up with everything they want to say in tiny font and then read it to the students – not a great strategy. If you are using PowerPoint, practice using it as key ideas for students and a prompt for you. Be ready to elaborate from there.

"Lectures continue to be one of the most commonly used teaching methods in higher education. An effective lecturer should aim to maximise the potential for student learning while stimulating motivation, giving students the opportunity and time to reflect on their beliefs and attitudes and to encourage further enquires. Lectures should not be used to transmit information that the students can acquire, often more effectively, from reading their textbooks. Unfortunately, this is the way they are most often used." (UTS website)

"Effective preparation involves developing an easy and straightforward structure by which you can match your aims and objectives within that time frame. It does not mean spending endless hours trying to get every single detail right and in doing so giving yourself high blood pressure." (UTS website)

A second mistake new lecturers often make is speaking too quickly. They have prepared so much material and they think they need to get through it all, rather than focusing on whether students are understanding what they are trying to teach. The new lecturer ends up breathless and the students end up frustrated. A few key points well explained and well illustrated will be a better experience for both parties. With practice you will learn how much can be covered in a lecture and how to speed up or slow down to fit the allotted time smoothly.

It might take some time to find your feet and work out your teaching style. Institutions offer courses and qualifications in tertiary teaching. Taking these is a good way to enhance your skills. The tertiary teaching facilitators will often be willing to observe your teaching and give feedback.

> *"Try to get stability in your teaching. I'd say to expect that the first 2 years are going to be tough when trying to develop new material and lectures but if you can get stability in teaching the same course then this will free up a significant amount of time for other aspects of scholarship."* (JM, early career academic)

How do you incorporate skill development?

One of the aspects of undergraduate teaching, especially with first year students, is that you are not just teaching content but also introducing the necessary academic skills. You might need to teach the academic style for essays or reports. You will almost certainly have to teach your discipline's referencing conventions. You will not be left on your own here. Your subject librarians will be very happy to run a session on using the library (both physically or electronically) and how to use the required referencing system.

If students have recently come from high school they will have learned some of these skills using supporting templates and exemplars. Our job is to get them to be a little more independent. Your teaching and learning centre will also help you here. (Return to Chapter 6 for ideas to assist students to plan and write essays.) Your institution might also have First Year Experience or other study workshops for students.

> *"According to students, good teachers:*
> - *want students to learn, and master the content;*
> - *want students to develop critical thinking skills;*
> - *display empathy;*
> - *encourage student feedback; [and]*
> - *are approachable outside classes."* (UTS website)

One approach that I have used in a variety of ways is the 'city—suburb—street' structure. The 'city' is the big idea that underpins the essay or exam question and provides the platform for the answer. The 'suburbs' are the sections that the answer will be divided into. These might be reasons, steps in an argument, sub-themes or key concepts. The 'streets' are the evidence, data, literature or examples that support the ideas in the suburbs.

I get students to use this as brainstorming and planning tool so that they are not just pouring everything they know onto paper or their computers without logic or coherence. They can then use it to structure their essay or examination response.

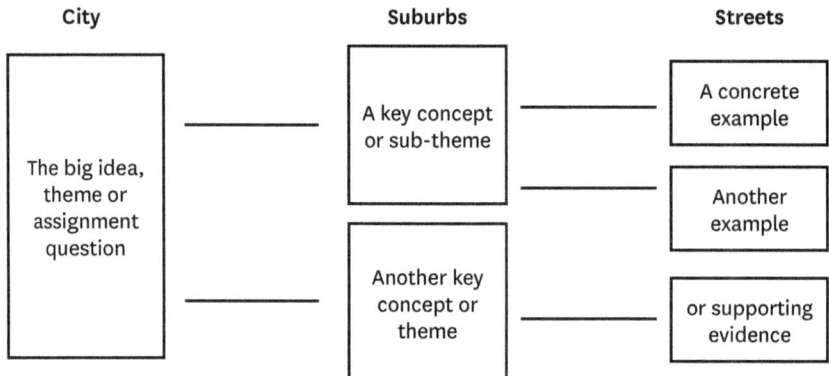

Here is an example of how this might work:

City	Suburbs	Streets
Discuss the ways in which globalisation has impacted on early childhood education	Theorists suggest globalisation consists of three global exchanges: Material exchanges (Economics) Power exchanges (Politics) Symbolic exchanges (Culture)	Examples in early childhood education in New Zealand are: Marketisation and the rise of 'for-profit' early childhood centres Impact of neoliberal concepts of individualism and 'parental choice' Emergence of kohanga reo/language nests as part of cultural revitalisation

What do you need to know about postgraduate teaching?

One of my early career academics is itching to get her own postgraduate course. I can understand that. The numbers are smaller, the atmosphere is more collegial and the conversations richer. That's probably one of the reasons why senior academics tend to hold on to their postgraduate courses. Postgraduate students usually come with a sound understanding of their discipline, stronger academic skills and a few more life experiences. Importantly, they are motivated enough to have made the choice to continue their studies at postgraduate level. This gives academics teaching the course the opportunity to go deeper into material that they are passionate about.

You might be lucky enough to start postgraduate teaching without needing to develop your own course and get it through all the institutional hurdles. It helps, however, to understand the differences between undergraduate and postgraduate teaching. Each of the points below might change how you approach your planning, teaching and assessment. These are broad generalisations, so remember that some third year students already think like postgraduates and some postgraduates, especially if they have had a break from study, might need more support.

Undergraduate teaching	Postgraduate teaching
• Is often an introduction to a discipline, profession or field • Often requires you to teach some of the discipline's skills and ways of thinking • Often requires an introduction to academic and referencing conventions • Is often to large groups in inflexible seating arrangements • Might include students from different year levels or disciplines • Is usually supported by tutorials or practical workshops • Might include field work or practice placements • Will usually have a smaller number of hours or credits • Might have a course text or set book of readings • Assignments are of shorter length (but due to group size you will have many more to mark) • Might include final examinations • Might be simulcast to other lecture rooms or campuses	• Usually requires a good pass (B or better) in prior study • Might have pre-requisites • Is usually a more intense exploration of a field, topic or discipline • Presumes students have a certain level of academic competence • Class size is usually smaller • Might include students from different undergraduate backgrounds • Courses are often longer and worth more credits • Individual sessions might be longer especially if they are taught in the evenings or as summer school intensives • Tutorials and practicals are not so common unless required for the programme accreditation • Readings are more conceptually and theoretically complex • Assignments are longer and require more knowledge, critique and depth • Might include a piece of independent student research

I invited one of our new academics to teach two sessions in one of my postgraduate courses. After her first session, I gave her some feedback. I suggested that she didn't need to stand and talk 'at' the postgraduates as she might do in her undergraduate lectures. As the group was small and the desks were in a horse-shoe shape, I advised her to sit and face them, use PowerPoint only as a discussion starter and speak in a more conversational and invitational tone. I encouraged her to address students by name and ask what they thought about the issue being discussed or to add their thoughts to an earlier comment. I suggested she relax and allow the discussion to evolve. She willingly took this advice and after her second session commented how much more she enjoyed the group and the different style and pace of teaching.

"When you teach, mean it. If you don't, you'll know, they'll know and nobody wins. If you do, you'll know, they'll know, and everybody wins." (DC, early career academic)

What is culturally responsive teaching?

By choosing to teach in Aotearoa New Zealand, you will be expected to integrate cultural considerations into your teaching. A culturally responsive approach is underpinned by some key assumptions:

- Both teachers and learners are culturally located.
- Both teachers and learners bring their own cultural perspectives and biases to the learning context.
- Teaching and learning are based on mutual respect.
- Culture should be celebrated and viewed as an asset in the learning context.
- Teachers need to be aware of their position of power and privilege.
- Deficit thinking and cultural stereotyping are not to be tolerated.

"It is about keeping culturally responsive and relational pedagogy in our minds all the time. We believe in relationships, caring, knowing them as culturally located human beings. We also believe in hard caring. There's no watering down of things. There's obviously culture there but cultural learning is not more important than the academic success, it's part of the academic success." (Kia Eke Panuku)[9]

While Māori students are meeting with more success in tertiary environments, especially since the advent of wānanga, many still feel alienated in traditional tertiary contexts. It is important for new academics to consider how they will acknowledge the role that culture plays in their classrooms. If you are new to or unfamiliar with Māori history, language and culture then it is important that you find a cultural mentor and undertake some professional development to expand your knowledge and understanding.

Understanding key Māori concepts and their relationship to the teaching and learning context is one place to start. Here are some to get you started. While grounded in te ao Māori, these ideas cross all cultural boundaries and can only improve the teaching and learning relationship:

Mannaakitanga	This means looking after others. In what ways will you welcome, nourish and support your students?
Whanaungatanga	This means creating a family-like atmosphere. In what ways will your students get to know and feel comfortable with you and each other?
Ōritetanga	This is about equity. How will you ensure your practices are equitable and the focus of your teaching enhances equitable outcomes for society?
Ako	This is the reciprocal nature of teaching and learning. In what ways will you show yourself as a learner as well as a teacher?
Whakamana	This is empowerment. How will you empower your students to achieve their goals through your teaching and their learning?
Mana motuhake	This relates to autonomy. How will you support your students to take responsibility for their learning and their future decision-making, especially in relation to their cultural aspirations?

The government has a strategy for enhancing Māori educational success. Called *Ka Hikitia*, it sets out goals and strategies at all levels of the education system. At the tertiary level it notes: "We want to increase the expectations of Māori students, which may require us to question how we think about teaching and learning. On the other hand, we want to enable whānau, iwi, Māori organisations and communities to influence and expect tertiary providers to be responsive to their needs in order to improve educational and labour market outcomes for Māori students."

"Ka hikitia! Ka hikitia!
Encourage and support!
And raise it to its highest level!
Ensure that high achievement is maintained
Hold fast to our Māori potential
Our cultural advantage
And our inherent capability
Nurture our young generation
The leaders of the future
Behold, we move onwards and upwards!"
(Ka Hikitia)[11]

Your institution will have support programmes for Māori learners, probably a marae or another place for them to get together, and mentors to support them. You can find out who the mentors are, build a relationship with them and find out how you can support Māori students in your classes. Our faculty, for example, has Te Korowai Atawhai (the cloak of kindness, warmth and support). Our university also offers a Tuākana programme. You could at least take time to get to know the Māori staff on your campus, attend pōwhiri, learn te reo and find out how to pronounce students' names and place names correctly.

> "Tuākana: It offers small-group learning, whakawhanaungatanga, wānanga, fonotaga, face-to-face meetings and workshops. These help connect Māori and Pacific students with senior Māori and Pacific students (tuākana), academic teaching staff, and key people across the University. Most Māori and Pacific students engage with Tuākana. They are supported by dedicated staff and meeting spaces with students often developing their own programmes to complement the teaching and learning environment." (UoA website)[12]

Another group of students who can find the traditional academic environment alienating are students from the many Pacific Islands that have made Aotearoa New Zealand their home. While these students might be grouped together and called 'Pasifika', this name belies the fact that they are from many different cultures, speak diverse languages and may be third or fourth generation New Zealanders. There is also a government strategy to improve Pasifika educational success called the *Pasifika Education Plan*. The same key principles apply to getting to know your Pacific students as your Māori students. Avoid making stereotypical judgments. Allow them to introduce themselves and tell you how they wish to be known and greeted as a step towards building a respectful and reciprocal relationship.

More often that not your class will be made up of many different cultures, representing a variety of countries of origin, languages, religions and beliefs. As you get to know your students, you can find ways to connect with them through your choice of examples, readings and resources. Be aware that your international students, who might come from very different academic environments, might take some time to adjust to our ways of doing things.

You can ask your students about their experiences, ideas and how they'd like the class to start. In my smaller undergraduate and postgraduate classes, I sometimes ask my students to take turns opening the session. They might choose a karakia, a poem, a prayer in their own language, a whakataukī, a proverb, a quote from a theorist or a wise saying. This way we acknowledge that we all have different backgrounds but for this class we come together to support each other in our learning endeavours. This week I am starting with John Marsden's poem *Prayer for the 21st Century*, which although written 20 years ago is chillingly relevant today.[13]

Before we leave talking about culturally responsive teaching, it is important to extend the same care and thoughtfulness to interactions with students and staff whose gender, sexuality, socio-economic background, ability/disability, politics, religion or beliefs are different to your own. Don't make assumptions about them. Get to know them and find out more about their lives, especially if they represent a group traditionally marginalised in academia. Be aware also of the status and power you hold and use these wisely and sensitively.

How might you teach in more innovative formats?

Finally, while most of the advice in this chapter has been about teaching in traditional formats and settings, you are just as likely to find yourself teaching on-line, using a blended format, teaching in a computer-assisted learning space, using 'clickers', 'flipping' your teaching or using any number of new approaches. You will certainly find many of your administrative forms, course books, set readings, assignment submission processes or plagiarism checking tools in digital formats. Your institution will have enthusiastic early adopters. If you are one of these find out what is available and begin by setting up your courses using the latest technology. You will need to get some local advice about platforms, facility bookings, funding for new technologies, IT protocols and technology support. You should also inquire about staff workshops.

"Thank you for Thursday's class. I really enjoyed it, and was thrilled to be able to identify the ideologies and their rhetoric by the end of the session. I also really appreciated the whakataukī at the start of the session to remove the layers from the day before entering into the learning for the evening. It really helped me to put my baggage aside and enjoy the learning." (MN, Postgraduate student)

"The revolution, although quiet, has not gone unnoticed and has led to justifiable claims that tertiary courses that focus on up-skilling teachers must appreciate the interconnection of ethnicity, power and privilege, while at the same time be active and intrinsically motivational. This requires the courses and those who run them to be acutely aware of the lived realities of their tertiary students' culture, be cognisant of the fact that knowledge should be co-created by educator and student and by student and student, and be accepting of the notion that an ongoing critique of power relationships within the tertiary contexts should prevail." (AM, senior academic)[14]

It is important to consider how using a different format changes the nature of your pedagogy and your relationships with your students. Don't assume that distance, on-line, blended, intensive or traditional formats can be easily substituted for each other, they each have their advantages and disadvantages.

If new technologies and formats are a bit overwhelming, find out what you are required to adopt and what is optional. Become familiar with the important ones, such as student management systems, digitised course materials or assignment grading tools. Then, as you set up your first courses, save templates and shortcuts that you can use with other courses. As you get more comfortable with what you are doing you can begin to experiment. Remember that the most important aspect of your teaching is not for the technology to take over your teaching but to enhance the student learning experience.

> "Many new staff have stated that they initially felt overwhelmed by time constraints. This was especially true when preparing classes. Task allocation and prioritising work is very important. Be strict with your time allocation and remember that when it comes to class delivery it's quality not quantity that counts. You will soon develop your own method of time allocation. Some have suggested that new staff may like to use a timetable at first before settling into a more informal routine." (UTS website)

Two of the innovations I have experimented with are on-line teaching and flipped teaching. For my research methods online course I used a computer programme that allowed me to have a structured lesson format with embedded video clips, reading links and online quizzes. I called this approach WRAP (watch/read/apply/ponder).

<u>Watch</u>: Students began by watching a short video clip of me introducing the key ideas for that session.

<u>Read</u>: They then read the relevant chapter from the text, *Doing Educational Research* (Mutch, 2005/2013).

<u>Apply</u>: The third task was to complete an interactive on-line quiz or activity that applied these ideas.

<u>Ponder</u>: The final aspect was writing an entry in their on-line research journal. Each student was also supported individually by phone or Skype as needed.

When my school offered a re-sit course for students in a professional programme who could not graduate without passing this compulsory course, I adapted my WRAP approach to flipped teaching. Flipped teaching is based on the idea that we spend too much time providing students with information that they could easily find themselves. Our role as teachers should focus instead on helping them process and apply this knowledge. I used the archived podcasts from the first semester's offering of the course. I called this approach L-RAP (listen/read/apply/prepare). (1) <u>Listen:</u> Before they came to class, students were to listen to the assigned podcast. (2) <u>Read:</u> They then read the assigned reading using the guiding questions. (3) <u>Apply</u>: They were to complete the online quiz. (4) <u>Prepare:</u> They then had time assigned to prepare their assignment portfolio.

When students came to class, we taught it in a workshop style, unpacking the readings and engaging students in processing activities and more in-depth discussion. It was win-win for everyone.

"Having the recorded lecture was great. I had a few days to get it done. Both lecturers were easy to understand and I really enjoyed the thoughtful conversations." (Undergraduate student)

Chapter 8 Building a research platform

Ka pū te ruha, ka hao te rangatahi

As an old net withers another is remade

- How do you use your earlier work as a platform for developing your research trajectory?
- How do you develop new or complementary areas of research?
- How do you seek funding for further or new research?
- How do you keep up your research momentum?

How do you use your earlier work as a platform for developing your research trajectory?

For many new academics, their PhD study is the platform for their research direction. Certainly the research undertaken to complete the doctoral degree requirements has ensured that you are well-grounded in the literature in the field, have a sound grasp of at least one appropriate methodology and have enough material for several publications, possibly even a book.

The hard part is sustaining the impetus. You might feel the need to take a break or diverge from your topic. You might be unable to gain further funding to continue in the same direction or you might secure a position that takes you away from the area you are most familiar with.

My advice is, if at all possible, try not to stray too far from your doctoral study. You have built up a substantial understanding of the field and your findings have added a new element. As you publish from your doctorate, you are beginning to establish yourself in this field. This is a sound basis from which to build a profile and to apply for further funding. Chapters 9 and 10 have advice for publishing from your thesis; this chapter focuses on building your research platform from your earlier research.

Once your thesis is completed and examined, you can start to think about it differently. Don't underestimate what a significant piece of work it was. It was carefully scrutinised by your supervisors and rigorously evaluated by your examiners. Publications arising from your thesis will further establish its worth. A good idea is to prepare a statement that does it justice so a potential funder gets a sense of what was accomplished. Here is an example:

Instead of: My thesis explored the provision of pastoral care to international students in New Zealand universities.	Say something like: My most recent research was a large mixed-method study of the provision of pastoral care to international students in New Zealand universities. It involved a survey of over 1,500 international students in five universities, 15 in-depth semi-structured interviews with international student support staff, five non-participant observations of international student induction programmes, seven student group interviews and analysis of 70 online and hardcopy policy and programme documents. The findings highlighted the areas that were not being fully addressed. The recommendations have led to policy and practice changes in the field.

You have some choices to make. Will the research direction you have begun sustain your long-term interest and help you achieve your goals? If not, how easy is it move to another field? How do you keep up momentum while you find a job, move cities or cope with other issues facing you in your life now your thesis is finished?

One interim solution is to build on your earlier research. Here are some ideas:

- Your thesis was time-bound. Your research had to stop in order to be examined, whether you felt you had exhausted the topic or not. There must be several

"Remember why you're doing it. You need to build time in for doing the things that made you happy to be an academic in the first place. This means being strict about not letting teaching or admin expand to fill the time available, and leaving space to get on with research (or vice versa). There's no point in having the job you love if you don't actually love doing it. That balancing act is going to be tricky—but it's all part of the learning curve." (LG, early career academic)

unexplored avenues that time did not allow you to investigate. Is there one that is relatively easy to continue with, that might not require too much funding to get started?

- Your thesis will probably have concluded with recommendations for further research. This is a good place from which to launch your ongoing research direction. Use one or more of your recommendations to make an argument for continued or new funding. From your knowledge of the literature you can probably support your argument with recommendations from other researchers in the field who have said similar things.
- Did your examiners raise questions that suggest a problem still to be examined or a possible direction in which to take your study?
- With your knowledge of the relevant research literature in the field, are there opportunities to extend what you have done by connecting your research to other findings, using your research to build onto what is already in the field to extend it further or to begin conducting a comparative study in another setting or with a different group of participants?

How do you develop new or complementary areas of research?

There might be circumstances that take you away from your thesis topic or discipline, such as winning a post-doctoral fellowship or lecturing position only tangentially related to your field. It will take time to rebuild your knowledge and expertise in the new field. It might require you to think outside the square so you don't lose momentum. Here are some questions that might help make links to capitalise on what you have already done:

> *"Rather than focusing on your career, focussing on your work creates a path. That means being flexible and open to opportunities rather than closing down what you do because of some pre-planned path."*
> (PO, senior academic)

Is there a relationship between your prior work and this new direction—for example, do they occur in the same setting, use a similar methodology or extend the same theory?

- How much of the various bodies of literature (substantive, methodological or theoretical) can be used to inform your new direction?

- Can you use your prior work to inform, extend or hold your new field up to scrutiny (or vice versa?)

When you move to a new field, it takes time to become known and for opportunities to come your way. Remember how long it took you to come to grips with your thesis field? You have experience under your belt now so this shouldn't take quite as long. You could:

- undertake some further postgraduate study in the new field
- attend seminars and conferences related to the new field
- read the key journals or important writers in the field
- introduce yourself to other academics in your institution working in the new field—and if you have moved institutions, you might also wish to touch base with those in your prior field
- use the literature review skills you honed in your prior study to build up a new literature base
- join the field's association and become part of the academic and/or practice community.

How do you go about seeking funding for new or further research?

In some fields, where scholarship is more philosophical or conceptual, seeking funding might not be such an urgent issue for you. In fields where research requires equipment, materials, computer programmes, analysis packages, buyout of your teaching, travel, contracting others, or giving koha, you need to become familiar with your institution's systems and timelines for tapping into funding. Most importantly, you don't need to do this alone. There will be people whose roles are to assist you to gain further funding and you can do this as part of a team or by cross-institutional collaboration. Here are some ways to get you started:

- Take advantage of the many opportunities for early career grants, such as Marsden Fast Start grants. There is usually a time limit, for example, 5–8 years since your doctorate was conferred, so don't wait too long. Your faculty or institution will usually have similar grants. Contact the people responsible for administering these to assist you with your application.
- Get to know the various funds available and their closing dates. Join a database or alerting service that keeps you up-to-date with funding

proposal calls. Introduce yourself to the person in the research office or your faculty who notifies academic staff of such calls.

- Attend the various funding roadshows, such as Marsden, Health Research Council, National Science Challenges or Ako Aotearoa to get a sense of how these operate and where your research direction might fit.
- Team up with others in your department or field, especially more experienced researchers, to be part of larger funding bids. It might mean that you end up doing the work for someone else so make sure that you have negotiated some authorship, conference attendance or research acknowledgement as part of the deal.
- Contact the person in your institution who seeks funding from philanthropic sources. There just might be a funder interested in your idea. Make sure you get support to build a convincing argument as to why this research needs to continue to be funded.

What is expected in a research funding proposal (RFP)?

Depending on your discipline, you might be part of larger funding bids put together by the leader of your research centre or you might have to put these together by yourself. It can be very daunting if you don't know where to start or what is expected. Here are some tips to get you started:

- Become familiar with your institutions online research funding application systems.
- Become familiar with the formats required for departmental, faculty or institutional funds.
- Start gathering the information required in the typical word limits. Give, for example, a two-page CV or a statement of your prior research (as discussed earlier in this chapter).
- Ask your mentor or research funding officer for exemplars of successful applications (be aware they might not always be forthcoming).
- Have a practice run through some of the easier formats—especially the online platforms they use. This way you'll be prepared for the questions that might trip you up at a later date when you are pushed for time—and this will inevitably happen, as timeframes for proposals are usually very tight.

- Budgets are one of the trickiest aspects of RFPs, so get familiar with what is contained in budgets; for example, personnel costs are not just a proportion of salary but will include ACC and superannuation costs. (When you add in your institution's overheads you'll begin to see why your anticipated budget might not stretch very far.)
- If you are applying for a national or international fund, you may find that they have quite specific requirements that do not appear in other formats, so be prepared for a range of questions.

Once you are familiar with the information required for an RFP and you know when the calls are released and the applications due, you are ready to begin. A few more tips:

- Read the call carefully. Note who the fund is for, what the funder wants from successful bidders and what the limitations and requirements are. Are you eligible? Do you have the expertise or prerequisites? Do you have the time? Would it be approved by your line manager?
- Note the process you might go through. Are they asking first for an Expression of Interest (EoI)? Will there be a shortlisting process? When is the full proposal due? Will there be interviews? When will you know if you are successful or not?
- Note the submission date. Plan your time backwards from there. Note if you need to submit it to your Head of Department or Research Office for approval ahead of that submission date. Give yourself plenty of buffer time—it will always take you longer than you think.
- Discuss your ideas and costs with your research office and financial officer well ahead of time and take their advice on board.
- Discuss your ideas with experienced researchers or others who have been successful with this fund.
- If your project involves others get them on board early and build their ideas into your planning. Do you (or they) need to get permission from their line managers or institutions?
- In general, your RFP will be similar to a research proposal (for example, the one you put together for your thesis) but it will include other aspects, such as the research team's experience and

the proposed budget. It might also include aspects you had not anticipated, such as how you will include Māori perspectives or what your dissemination plan will be.

- Be prepared for disappointment. Your application will possibly face fierce competition from other bidders. RFPs take a long time to put together and your possible lack of success might dampen your motivation. I have about a one in five success rate. When I'm not successful, I pick myself up and start again using as much from prior unsuccessful RFPs as I can. Eventually you will be successful.

How do you keep up your research momentum?

In your new career, you will be overwhelmed by new things—new people, possibly a new institution and a new city. Even if you are familiar with this institution, you are in a new role. You are expected to attend meetings, complete paperwork, prepare and teach your own classes, become familiar with policies and procedures—*and* keep up your research. My best advice is to try not to do more than is necessary until you have established a routine and a balance that works for you. I know you want to make your mark but it will be better to be known as someone who does several things well rather than someone who makes promises they can't keep or always does a rushed job. Take your time. Attend to the basics. Plan out what is achievable. Set some time aside to regularly engage with your research, even if it is in small bursts, such as reading articles, searching for funding opportunities, planning new projects or sharing your findings at a seminar. Once you are settled into a more stable routine you can set larger blocks of time aside and re-engage more fully with your research endeavours.

> **"Read!** I try and read one scientific paper every working day of the year. It's hard, and doesn't always happen. Indeed, it's closer to 3-4 per week. But I find it helps me to keep abreast of the literature, and I feel like I'm up with current ecological discussions. That makes my job as a reviewer, grant applicant, advisor, lecturer easier - because I know where my discipline is at." (JM, mid-career academic)

Chapter 9 Organising a writing plan

He kai kei aku ringa

There is food at the end of my hands

- How do you maximise your earlier efforts?
- What do you include in an abstract?
- How do you set up a writing plan?
- How do you keep up momentum?

How do you maximise your earlier efforts?

It is very satisfying to receive a copy of your first peer-reviewed publication. I remember the pride of my senior colleagues as they congratulated me on this milestone. What I soon learned, however, was that as one article came to publication, I needed to add another one to the production line. This chapter aims to help you make the best of what you already have and to keep your publications flowing.

Let's start with what you already have. I'm anticipating that you have a completed thesis and possibly some unpublished conference presentations. The first thing that you must do is get advice. Each discipline or field has its own conventions. Some fields value books that establish your original contribution; others prefer articles in international peer-reviewed journals. Some measure your contribution by your sole or lead authorship; others expect that you will publish collaboratively. Once you have established which outlets are best for you it is time to review what you have and decide where to start.

A quick way to get runs on the board is to start with pieces that are already completed but might just need extending or updating. Begin with extended abstracts you prepared for conferences or a conference paper that was not published in conference proceedings. Here is a helpful procedure to follow, which will set up a good routine for the future.

> "It is obvious to anyone who has spent any time around a university that getting published is a good way of increasing our chances of winning scholarships and having research grants approved. Moreover, a healthy publication record will also increase our chances of being promoted and, in the worst-case scenario, will help us hold onto those jobs when budget cuts call for departmental downsizing"
> (CD & NL, senior academics)[15]

1. Review the piece critically—what is the key message or argument? What are the strengths of the piece? What aspects need further work?
2. Ask your mentor or critical friend for their advice on what you might do with the piece and where you might submit it.
3. Check out the outlets in your field. Are you interested in regular journal issues, special journal issues, book chapters in edited books or contributing to a monograph series?
4. Read other pieces in these outlets. Who is the target audience? What style is preferred? What topics are covered? Which theories, methodologies or data analysis and presentation strategies regularly appear? What instructions are given to authors?
5. Look for articles, chapters or books in the series that relate to your topic and include some of these in your literature review or discussion. This signals to the editor that you are aiming for a similar audience.
6. Use the strategy suggested in Chapter 6 where you start with the word limit and then divide the sections into achievable chunks. Allocate time to each section. If you are working on a piece that is already near completion, this shouldn't need too much time.
7. Remember to take time to polish, proofread and check the accuracy of the references.
8. When you feel it is finished, give it back to your mentor or critical friend for their final feedback. Then send it off to your chosen outlet and wait for their decision (see Chapter 10 for the editorial and review process).

A point to note—avoid self-plagiarism—this is when you repackage and republish your own material without substantially changing it. As a young academic I was told that not more than 30 per cent of a new piece should be drawn from your prior publications and that 30 per cent should not be easily recognisable. It should be rewritten to suit the new audience and publication outlet.

The second way you can get material off to the publishers quickly is to draw on your thesis. If you are planning to turn it into a book, this will take a little longer—and I talk about that in the next chapter. Below I am suggesting that you examine your thesis for how many ways you might divide it up. With care and thought you could make four or five different pieces. Here are some suggestions:

> *"Get published early in a good journal."* (GM, early career academic)

The study in summary form	This is your typical journal article. It has an introduction, summarised literature review, brief theoretical or conceptual framework, findings, discussion and conclusion. It can go to a journal in your field. Highlight what your article adds to the field and suggest further research or policy implications.
The methodology	If your methodology was in any way innovative or problematic, it might be of interest to a methodological journal, such as a qualitative, quantitative, mixed methods, arts-based, narrative inquiry or case study journal. Focus on what other users of this method could learn from your experiences.
The theoretical framework	There are many journals that focus on exploration, use or adaptations of current theories that discuss or critique the ideas of major theorists. They might be outside your discipline so check how your work suits a more philosophical interpretation in a field you are less familiar with.
Any ethical or practical issues you faced	There are also journals that focus on research ethics or the practicalities of research. You might also find auto-ethnographic journals where you can bring your research journey and the findings together in one piece.
Taking sections from your findings or discussion and expanding	If you had several discussion chapters, such as individual cases or themes, these could be repackaged for different outlets (see my example of how I have divided up my research into schools in disaster settings later in this chapter). You will need to rewrite the introductions and conclusions to suit.
Re-analysing data	Sometimes, often because of time limitations when finishing your thesis, you needed to stay with the analytic tool that you began with but you are left wondering 'what if?' If your raw data would suit re-analysis with a different statistical method or theoretical analysis, this expands your publication possibilities.

What do you include in an abstract?

One of the things I find my doctoral students struggle with, both when preparing their theses for examination, when writing up parts of their theses for publication or preparing an extended abstract for a conference, is what goes in an abstract. While abstracts have varying word limits, the following advice I've given my students might be a good place for you to get started. The skill of writing an abstract is also helpful in training you to keep your focus when you write longer pieces. Of course, once you've addressed these aspects you can rearrange it to make it flow better and engage the reader's interest.

What to include in an abstract
1. Opening sentence that says exactly what the piece is about without any fluff. *This thesis/article/presentation …*
2. Explain to the reader what the problem or issue is and why it is of interest at this time. *In times of …, it is important that …*
3. Summarise the literature and show where your research fills a gap or elaborates on a particular aspect. *The literature in this field … but …*
4. Provide your research question as a link to the next section of the thesis. *The research addresses this by …*
5. Explain what philosophical, theoretical or conceptual framework underpins the thesis. *The research is situated in …*
6. Show how the methodology flows naturally from your stated theoretical position and is coherent with the question you set out to answer. *The [chosen] research approach best answers …*
7. Briefly introduce the research sources, sample size, and ethical considerations. *This research was undertaken…*
8. Introduce the analytic framework (that is how you made sense of the data). *The data were analysed using …*
9. Discuss the key findings, their significance and implications. *The key findings were …*
10. Conclude with the unique contribution that your research makes to the field. *In conclusion, this research adds to the field by …*

How do you set up a writing plan?

Although tertiary institutions have suggested targets (which vary by level and discipline) for the number of peer-reviewed publications expected each year, due to the vagaries of the publication process, you need to have several on the go in order to meet these targets.

If, for example, you are expected to have two publications per year, then I suggest you have five at different stages of development. In order to keep track of my pieces in different stages of development, I prepare a writing plan. I predict the stage of each piece and fill in proposed completion dates working backwards from the due date. I also set this up as a monthly plan so I can mark out space in my diary for what I need to do for each of the pieces. This ensures that I keep up momentum and know where I am with each piece.

In the following chart I have used possible examples from my current research based on work with schools following the Canterbury earthquakes. You can see that some publications are more advanced than others:

"Find time to write. I really like writing (hence, the Blog) but almost feel like it is a luxury in my job. Time doesn't permit me to sit at my desk and just write. So, you need to find a way to write, and on a regular basis. I do that two ways. I try and write (or edit) for at least one hour of every second morning (first thing). I also try and work at home one day a fortnight. This mightn't seem much, but you'd be amazed how quickly a month flies by without having worked on a paper when you've got teaching on, grading or thesis examinations to do."

(JM, mid-career academic).

Topic: Role of schools in disasters	Possible outlet	Idea development	Ethical clearance and research plan	Data gathering and analysis	Draft	Peer feedback and revision	Submission to journal	Under review	Revision re-submission
Principals as crisis managers	Journal of Leadership Studies	→							
Teachers as first responders	Teachers and Teacher Education		→						
Children's emotional responses	Pastoral Care in Education				→				
Schools as community hubs	The School Community Journal						→		
Post-disaster school closures	Aust. Journal of Disaster & Trauma Studies								→

Note, this is only a *plan*. It needs constant adjustment as other commitments change your proposed timeframes. You might find an article is returned requiring major revisions or is rejected and you need to start again with another outlet. Having it plotted out like this helps you to adjust timeframes, rethink priorities and reset deadlines.

You might work better with a plan that puts a date on when you anticipate (or need) to complete each task. Here is the same plan set out across several months. This enables you to plan your writing around busy teaching times, leave or other commitments:

2017	January	February	March	April	May ...
Principals as crisis managers		Ethical approval due Feb 11 ✓	Work on lit review		Contact potential participants
Teachers as first responders		Complete analysis by Feb 15	Organise article structure		
Children's emotional responses	Send to critical friend ✓		Revise and proofread		Submit to *PCE* by May 15 deadline
Schools as community hubs	Submit to *SCJ* ✓			Check status	Attend to revisions
Post-disaster school closures		Revision due to AJDTS 28 Feb ✓		Check proofs	Publication :)

Don't forget to celebrate each piece that makes it all the way publication. This is not achieved lightly and you deserve to reward yourself (even if it's just a smiley face on your writing plan) and thank your supporters for helping you get there.

How do you keep up writing momentum?

In the previous chapter, I talked about keeping up the momentum in your research. You will face the same dilemma with keeping up your writing. Teaching manages to take care of itself because you can't leave a class of anxious students to fend for themselves. Writing, however, is harder to manage. It requires self-discipline to put aside all possible distractions and get on with it. My best advice is to treat writing as you would any other appointment. Put it in your diary. Say that you are unavailable. Write in the place with the least distractions. It might be in your office with a note on your door asking to not be interrupted or it might be at home while your partner is at work and your children are at school. Here are some suggestions:

"Only a fortunate few find that good writing comes quickly, easily and pleasurably. Some find writing a slow and painful struggle that they often avoid. Most academics find that it is neither especially difficult nor easy: it is just routine labour which has to be done." (CD & NL, senior academics)

"My advice: To always set aside time for writing. There is a limitless amount of time that you can put into your teaching so it is about ensuring that you block off time for developing your articles, ideas and reading." (JM, early career academic)

- Check your timetable for teaching, meetings and other commitments. Block out chunks of time. Smaller chunks, such as an hour or so, are more suitable for keeping up with reading, planning a piece or attending to revisions. For focused writing you might need longer stretches of time from a half day for a particular aspect to a week or more for intense writing and refining.
- State what you will do in the allotted time by prioritising from your publication plan. Cover all the different aspects of writing—reading, planning, writing, revising or proofreading.
- Before you leave one writing session, take time to prepare for the next. Leave yourself a note of things you had completed, things you need to attend to before the next writing session and things that you anticipate achieving in the next session.
- Divide up your allocated time. Very few people sit at their desk and write solidly for hours without a break. Plan to include time for thinking, reading, revising as well as fresh writing. Set yourself some achievable targets. It might be a particular task or a number of words.
- Find your natural rhythm. Do you need to start by reading over what you wrote last time or do you want to get your new ideas down before you lose them? How long at a stretch can you write without losing focus? How often do you need to take a micro-break?
- Aim to get underway quickly. Do you need to arrange your desk, put on music, shut the dog outside or prepare drinks and snacks? Get these things out of the way so they don't become distractions.

One of the reasons that many novice writers can't get started is that they are crippled by the idea that their first draft must be perfect. A first draft is simply that: *a first draft*. Expect that you will rewrite and recraft several times and build this into your timetable. Don't let perfection get in the way of getting started or finished. Also don't think of writing as a solitary activity. Find some writing buddies. You might join a writing support programme, such as "How to write an article in 12 weeks" or "Shut up and write" or you might just touch base with a friend to discuss what you have done and aim to do. Do you remember how knowing you had a supervision meeting coming up improved your focus and output?

Finally, enjoy writing. It is such an important part of an academic's life. It should provide both intrinsic and extrinsic rewards. Find ways in which the art of writing or the act of completion provides you with the warm satisfaction of a job well done.

Chapter 10 Preparing for publication

Nō he kākano iti, e puawai ana he kauri

From a small seed, a tall tree will blossom

- How do you get published?
- How do you turn your thesis into a book?
- How do you choose your dissemination outlets carefully?
- How do you determine authorship?
- What is a typical publishing process?
- How do cope with rejection?

How do you get published?

My first piece of advice is to have something worthwhile to say. If it is reporting an empirical study, it will need to have clearly articulated methods and trustworthy data, be accurately displayed and present new knowledge. If it is a more conceptual piece, it will have to be well written, convincingly argued and present a new perspective. I recently reviewed a piece where the data were gathered in one field but interpreted through a theoretical lens from another field. I wasn't sure if the authors could pull this off but they did. They showed they knew the context and literature of both fields, they set out their argument clearly and used their data to get the reader to think about the problem and possible solutions in quite a different way. I felt it was definitely worth publication.

My second piece of advice is to match your message to your audience and say it in an engaging way. The clearest outline I know of what a publishable paper should contain comes from a 'pocket guide' written in the 1990s which seems to me have stood the test of time. The authors (Kenway, Gough & Hughes, 1998) state:

The papers most likely to get published will:

- present new knowledge
- demonstrate a thorough knowledge of the particular field
- address the current issues which the field confronts
- ask, and at the least, attempt to answer provocative questions in a persuasive manner
- bring new insights to current debates and issues
- be well written and argued; and
- know what appeals to particular journals and readers.

> *"The intellectual authority of academia is largely premised on the fact that it is a public activity. This means that our research needs to be placed in a context where it is open to scrutiny by colleagues. This process provides a check on the logic of our reasoning and works against us letting our egos get in the way of our work. This is one way our knowledge progresses; we do our research and publish our results, and then others in the academic community (or outside it) may point out its shortcomings or argue for alternative explanations."*
> (CD & NL, senior academics)

The authors (Kenway et al.) also have a further useful set of guidelines on what makes a piece theoretically adequate, methodologically adequate, analytically adequate and stylistically adequate. This is a useful checklist for your own writing or when you are asked to review the writing of others:

Each publishable paper has its own internal consistency and coherence. It will be:
- Theoretically adequate
    The theoretical perspective is clear and focused.
    The concepts used are clearly defined.
    The findings relate to the research literature presented in the article.
    The conclusions are a logical consequence of the arguments presented in the paper.
- Methodologically adequate
    Sufficient information is given on how the research was undertaken.
    Rationale for the use of a particular methodology is clear.
    The data presented relate to the method.
    Title, abstract, literature review and text are all relevant to the argument.

- Analytically adequate
    - Is critical and analytic rather than descriptive.
    - Analysis supports theoretical claims.
    - Analysis is systematic.
- Stylistically adequate
    - Attention is given to referencing, grammar and punctuation.
    - Language is inclusive and non-sexist.
    - Abbreviations and acronyms are defined.
    - Any features local to the research site are explained for an international audience.

Source: Kenway, J. Gough, N. & Hughes, M. (1998). *Publishing in refereed academic journals: A pocket guide*, 1998, pp.5–6

How do you turn your thesis into a book?

If you are considering turning your thesis into a book, first talk to those in your field. You might start with your supervisor, mentor or a senior colleague experienced in publishing books. Ask them to give you frank advice about whether your book has publishing potential. It's not about quality; it's about whether a publisher will think your topic is saleable. Self-publishing or vanity publishing does not look good on your CV or promotion application, so if a reputable publisher cannot be found, it is better to turn your thesis into a series of journal articles.

"Publishing enables you to record for posterity your findings, your interpretations, your beliefs, your attitudes and whatever you care to include. Publications are like treasure houses of ideas that can be visited by others and revisited by the authors themselves. Publishing provides the world with a statement. The statement can be read by hardly any at all or by thousands of people. And publications do not grow old, although their content may date." (PS, senior academic)[16]

If you receive encouragement to go ahead, that does not mean your thesis can be turned automatically into a book. Your thesis was written to a set of academic conventions with your examiners in mind. You need to adjust your content and style for a different audience.

- Do you need to change the structure to something that is more engaging? A book doesn't usually follow the same structure as a thesis. You might, for example, need to summarise the theory and methodology sections to make them more palatable.
- Do you need to alter the level of detail? Too much detail might be overwhelming for a general audience. Too little detail, and your

audience might be left confused. Do you need to explain concepts or assumptions for a general audience that academics in your field usually take for granted?
- Is the level of language, that is, use of jargon, technical terms or acronyms, appropriate for your intended audience?
- What is the narrative thread that will hold the book together?
- Do you need to do any updating, amending or deleting?

Start with publishers whose books are common in your field. Spend time looking at their websites. What kind of books do they publish? Who are their target audiences? What advice do they give to authors? What do they expect in a book proposal? Check with others in your field if these are reputable publishers (see the following section on choosing your dissemination outlets).

You might like to talk to the publisher's representatives in person. You will often find them at conferences or you can phone or email for an initial appointment. If you get an interested response then you will probably need to prepare a book proposal. Each publisher will have their own expectations. The proposal for this book used the following headings. I make some suggestions alongside these headings:

Working title	Make your title engaging. Does it say what it's about in a catchy way without being dense or wordy? Does it have an easy-to-remember short form? Is it descriptive enough to be found by search engines?
Author details and biography	The publisher needs to know that you have expertise and/or qualifications in the field you are writing for. They also need a set of contact details that won't change while they are dealing with your manuscript.
Rationale for book	Why is your book necessary and timely? What gap or niche is it filling? What does it add to the field?
Proposed format	What genre or form will the book take? Is it an autobiographical journey? Is it a suitable as an introductory textbook? Will it contain illustrations, tables and graphs or pages of poetry?
Intended audience	Who is your target audience? Think about this carefully. If it is for scholars in your field it will be different to a book for a general audience. Don't try to cover every possibility in one book.
Market competition	What else is out there that is similar? Conduct a search on Amazon or ask your librarian to help you here. How is your book different? What does it re-interpret, enhance or critique?

Proposed chapters	Provide the book's structure in the form of chapter headings. For each chapter include a short description or abstract. You might even provide a sample chapter that you have worked on. Don't send in your entire thesis. Show how you will adapt it.
Tentative timeline	Be realistic about how long would it take you to shape up each chapter. Include time to have them peer-reviewed by a critical friend and for you to pull the whole book together, including proofreading, referencing and indexing.

How do you choose your dissemination outlets carefully?

New academics often receive advice about where to and where not to publish. It is important to get to know what is the norm in your field. The following table is a quick guide to the advantages and disadvantages of the most usual publication choices—but remember these vary across disciplines.

Type of outlet	Advantages	Disadvantages	Comments
Highly ranked peer-reviewed international journal	Shows you are at the top of your game. Looks good on CV and job applications.	High rejection rate. Might require complete revision and resubmission.	It might take some time to get to publication but it is worth the prestige.
Lower ranked but niche journal and/or regional or national journal	More likely to reach your target audience. More likely to be cited by researchers in similar fields.	Fine at very early or much later stages in your career but promotions committees want evidence of international impact.	A journal with an impact factor under 1.0 is not considered highly so you need to argue it has more impact other ways.
A sole authored book or monograph	Stamps your mark on the field. Best if it is published by reputable publisher.	Uses up all your good ideas/data in one go. You need to weigh up whether this would be better as multiple articles.	This very much depends on your field. Can be a long and onerous process depending on the publisher.
An edited book	Editing a book shows you have credibility in your field. Allows you to get a chapter (or two) of your own published.	You only get the credit in output terms for what is included as your own original peer-reviewed work (e.g., your chapter, but not your preface).	Depending on your contributing authors and your skill in managing them, this can be a quick and easy or long and fraught process.

Book chapters	Good for peer esteem if you have been invited to contribute. Often longer word length so you get to expand on your ideas.	Not viewed as highly as journal articles because the peer review process is not as definitive—important that you articulate this clearly.	As with authored or edited books, the process and timeframe to publication can vary markedly.
Textbook or book for a wider audience	Often consolidates many years of work in your field. Gets you known by your peers or wider readership. Is more likely to pay royalties.	Not viewed as highly as items listed above because it is either seen as (a) a synthesis of earlier work rather than new original work or (b) a lighter version of intellectual work.	Is probably more important to establish yourself through higher prestige outlets first (even if I personally think that writing for such audiences is quite a different skill that not everyone has).
On-line or digital format	Gets your work out there instantly. Gets you a following. You can easily get statistics on impact.	Harder to argue that it meets the peer-reviewed, quality assured criteria. You never know where your ideas go.	Best to do in conjunction with other outputs—you can use one to enhance the impact of the other.

Novice writers, in their anxiety to get published quickly, sometimes fall victim to what are called predatory publishers. These outlets might not peer review your work or they might charge an exorbitant fee. Work published in these forms is often effort wasted as they do not look good on your CV and might not count as high quality peer-reviewed outputs for promotion or PBRF purposes. Beall's List[17] of predatory publishers is a site that suggests publishers to avoid. In his 2016 list are over 900 "potential, possible, or probable predatory scholarly open-access publishers" and a further 800 stand-alone journals. Jocalyn Clark has a five-point plan to help researchers avoid predatory journals. Her advice is below:

1. Is the journal or publisher listed in Beall's List? If so, it should be avoided, as this "blacklist" is regularly updated and specifies criteria for identifying predatory journals and publishers.
2. If claiming to be an open access journal, is the journal in the Directory of Open Access Journals (DOAJ)? This is a sort of "whitelist," and journals here must meet specific criteria.
3. Is the publisher a member of recognised professional organisations that commit to best practices in publishing, such as the Committee on Publication Ethics (COPE); the International Association of Scientific, Technical, & Medical Publishers (STM); or the Open Access Scholarly Publishers Association (OASPA)?

4. Is the journal indexed? Do not accept the journal's claims about being indexed. Instead verify these claims by searching for the journal in databases such as PubMedCentral (free) or the Web of Science (requiring subscription).
5. Is the journal transparent and following best practices when it comes to editorial and peer review processes, governance, and ownership? Are there contact details for the journal and its staff (email, postal address, working telephone number)? Reputable journals have a named editor and editorial board comprised of recognised experts. Are the costs associated with publishing clear? Credible journals do not ask for a submission fee. Many bona fide open access journals require a publication charge, but this is levied after acceptance and through a process separate from the editorial process.

Source: http://blogs.bmj.com/bmj/2015/01/19/jocalyn-clark-how-to-avoid-predatory-journals-a-five-point-plan/

Many academics are also wary of open access but there are high quality journals that offer open access as an option, usually with a charge to recoup what they would lose from the loss of journal subscriptions. There are other journals that undertake open access as a matter of principle, without charge, in order to make research available to all, especially readers in developing countries without access to libraries or the financial capital to purchase journals or individual articles.

It's easy to become influenced by 'fads' about the right journals or publishers. I have found that the most effective way to develop a publishing profile is to publish where you know your work will be of value or make a difference." (JW, senior academic)

It is expensive to take up the open access option offered by top-level publishers but experienced academics factor this cost into their funding applications or willingly carry the cost themselves as it increases download and citation rates.

Often a journal will have both online and hardcopy versions. You might find your article online well before the issue of that journal is completed. This online version is still usually behind a paywall. Online publication dates have become important as they can be used as evidence of an article being published in a certain year, especially if this information is needed for applications, awards or research assessment exercises, such as PBRF. Note that some appointment and promotions committees are still wary of online publications so it is important that you can show that your open-access or online article was thoroughly reviewed and edited by a scholarly and reputable publisher or organisation.

How do you determine authorship?

This is a highly contentious question and one that varies across disciplines. In some fields, the leader of your research team or your doctoral supervisor expects to be an author on all publications related to the research you have done with them. In other fields, supervisors consider the work the student's own and only seek authorship if they write a section or make a reasonable contribution to the piece. You should ask what is expected in your field so you are not taken by surprise. You should also ask how the order of authors is determined. It might be that the person with the highest status comes first, or the person who did the most work, or it might be in alphabetical order (with a footnote to explain this), or your team might take turns at being first author. I find that, although the conversation can sometimes be awkward, it is best to determine this ahead of time and have all parties agree. It must be open to negotiation later on, however, if someone drops out or does not complete what was expected of them and someone else picks that extra work up. If you were only a research or editing assistant you are not generally considered an author but you might be mentioned in the acknowledgements at the end of the article.

What is a typical publishing process?

It can take anywhere between 6 months and 2 years for an article to go from submission to publication. I have had new academics tell me that they sent their article in 2 weeks ago and still haven't heard. I explain that the editor is usually doing this job on top of a full academic workload and has to fit it in where possible. Online submission processes mean that an article is easier to track but if you have sent it to an academic's email address and haven't heard after a month, then I'd follow up.

I have outlined below the usual process and a typical timeline but be patient, this can vary hugely:

Timeframe	Your involvement	Editor's tasks	Reviewers' involvement
1–3 months	Submission	Decision as to suitability Selection of reviewers Send out for review	
3–6 months		Decision based on reviewers' feedback	Reviews completed and returned
6–8 months	Revision	Accepted or returned to reviewers	Revised version reviewed
8–12 months	Check proofs	Accepted Sent for formatting Proofs returned to you	
12–24 months	Receive hard copy	Online copy uploaded Issue compiled Hardcopy published	

Reviewers are usually asked to respond to a set of criteria about relevance to the journal, research and writing quality and whether the article is comprehensible to an international audience. There might be two sections to complete, one with comments to the author and another with confidential comments to the editor (this allows a reviewer to be more blunt than they would be to an author). Finally, reviewers select a recommendation, for example: publish; publish with minor revisions; publish with major revisions; publish with major revisions and resubmit (to be reviewed again); or reject. The editor is the arbiter and communicates the decision to you with the full or edited reviewers' comments. Once the reviews are returned to you, you are expected to make the suggested changes (or explain why not). I usually do this in a table with the suggested revisions from each reviewer in the left-hand column and what changes I made (or not) as a result of that feedback on the right, noting the pages on which the changes can be found.

How do you cope with rejection?

Yes, it will happen. And, yes, it has happened to everyone I know. And, yes, it still hurts when it happens. As an academic you can often feel under constant measurement. Every course you teach is evaluated. Every year you undergo a performance appraisal. Committees are always deciding whether you will be appointed, promoted, given research and study leave, have your project funded, receive an award or obtain a reasonable PBRF rating. It feels the same with publishing and it seems unfair at times. Does a pastrycook have every pie examined by two judges before it is sold?

Your first feeling of rejection can come when your critical friend or mentor, who has been so encouraging to date, reads your submission and suggests some major improvements. In your state of pre-publication anxiety, try to view this positively as they really want you to succeed. Next, after you have sent it off to your chosen journal, it could be returned immediately by the editor for any number of reasons. It might not be suitable for the journal. It might not be written in their house style. It might be too long. The special issue call might have closed. Again, try not to take this to heart by thinking you are not good enough.

> "As an emerging researcher it can be challenging to publish your research knowing that you are putting your work out there for other academics to review. When I first started publishing I recall reading one reviewer's comments and thought there was no hope in this work. However, I have learned to grow a hard shell, I managed to refine my article and was pleased to have it later published."
>
> (JaM, early career academic)

If your article is sent out to reviewers, it might receive highly divergent reviews leaving the editor to make a hard decision. If your editor chooses 'major revision'—that is *not* rejection—it means that with the suggested changes it is suitable for publication in that journal.

If your editor chooses 'reject', there is nothing you can do, except read the feedback and use it to make appropriate improvements. Choose another journal and start the process all over again. Can you be rejected more than once? Yes, but take heart, JK Rowling's first Harry Potter book was rejected 12 times before being published. I have had an article rejected outright by one journal then accepted without revisions by another.

When I receive wildly differing reviews (or feedback that makes me wonder if the reviewer actually read my article), I shake my head in disbelief and groan about the peer review process. Despite its flaws, it is still the most widely accepted system for determining the quality of a piece of writing. When I receive feedback, I still feel my heart rate go up. I sigh with relief if the reviews are good. If they are mixed or not good, I read them quickly then put them away for a few days. This way I can read them again without emotion and can focus on how to use the advice to produce a better piece. As an editor, I often see the improvements when an article is revised and resubmitted. My best advice is to see the feedback as a gift to enable you to produce something you will be immensely proud of.

Finally, never forget how harsh feedback made you feel. When you become a reviewer treat the author as you would like to have been treated—acknowledge the good parts and make constructive suggestions in a supportive tone on any aspects that could be improved.

"I want to let you know how appreciative the chapter author was for your feedback. The email I received this morning said:
'Thank you for your message and for this lovely feedback. I am actually touched that [the reviewer] provided the guidance sheet as well, to illustrate her "signposting"—and yes, it is helpful. Sometimes, time and fresh eyes are quite helpful here!'" (Anonymous author and book editor)

Chapter 11 Undertaking supervisions

Waiho i te toipoto; kaua i te toiroa

Let us keep close together not wide apart

- Why is supervision important?
- What are the personal and professional benefits of supervision?
- What is expected of you as a supervisor?
- What do you do when issues arise?
- What is involved in examining theses and dissertations?

In this chapter, I focus on research supervisions. You may also be involved in practicum or clinical supervisions in fields such as education, social work or nursing but I discuss these in the next chapter in relation to service. I find research supervision one of the joys of being an academic. To use your expertise to assist someone to take their raw ideas and bring them to fruition through their research is such a rewarding thing to do. To see them walk across the stage at graduation knowing the back story of their achievement—the highs and lows, the roadblocks and the epiphanies—and to feel that you had a small part in their success is immensely satisfying.

"Formal academic supervision is an essential ingredient of doctoral study in our country. At this highest level of education, the underlying model is something like an apprenticeship in which a novice researcher (the student or candidate) learns through a close, 'almost hands-on' working relationship with one or more experienced researchers." (He Rautaki mo te Akoranga Kairangi)[18]

Why is supervision important?

Institutions of higher learning have as two of their cornerstones, the awarding of higher-level degrees and the creation of new knowledge. Indeed, funding regimes such as New Zealand's Performance-Based Research Fund (PBRF) measure success through degree completions, competitive research grants gained and publications in peer-reviewed outlets.

Most New Zealand universities follow the UK model of research degrees where a student is supervised closely by one or more supervisors with expertise in the field. At masters level there might be a programme of taught courses culminating in an independent piece of research, written up as a thesis or dissertation. In the sciences, this research might be part of a larger collaborative study, where the topic is assigned by the lead researcher. In the humanities, it is more likely to be a topic of the candidate's choice where the supervisors assist the candidate to follow a more independent direction.

At doctoral level, the most common model is a doctoral candidate working closely with two or more supervisors on a major piece of work over several years in which the candidate is inducted into academia through a close personal supervisory relationship. In this model, the candidate follows up an independent inquiry guided by one or more experienced academics in the field. They meet regularly as the research progresses until the supervisors feel the research has been conducted and written up to a standard ready for external examination.

External examination may be followed by an oral examination—a viva voce—before the degree is conferred. There are, of course, variations on this process—an oral presentation might be expected at the proposal stage rather than at the examination stage or both. A university might require a formal probation period in a candidate's first year culminating with formal presentation and a peer-reviewed proposal.

> *"I take research mentoring seriously. For me, research quality over quantity is paramount. I've never had more than six PhD students at any one time and I like this—it gives me time to be involved in their work at a meaningful level. That way, I can spend lots of time discussing their data, musing over experimental design, and getting to know them as individuals. I think the best thing I can do is invest my time in people and a small lab suits my hands-on style. It also allows me to do some of my own research too, and this keeps me sane."*
> (JM, mid-career academic)

There are other models available; for example, a professional doctorate, such as an EdD, which might combine taught courses and thesis production, more akin to the US model. One of the strengths of this model is the collaborative nature of the approach, in which a cohort of candidates moves through the degree together offering each other moral support in a way not often available in the independent research model. Another option, often suitable for academics already working in an institution of higher learning and expected to be publishing as part of their role, is PhD *by* or *with* publication. In this way publications produced during the candidature can be included in an annotated portfolio in place of a single thesis. Finally, creative PhD options are becoming more widespread. The creative element might be a performance or a collection of poetry with an exegesis (an accompanying theoretical or methodological elaboration) or the presentation of the thesis might use creative methods such as writing a novel or creating a collage. It is important as a new supervisor that you are familiar with the formats and expectations of your discipline. Experienced supervisors can show or talk you through examples.

The conferring of a doctoral degree and the right to use the title "Dr" recognises that the candidate has reached the exacting standard set by their discipline. As such, doctoral supervision is a serious business. You are the conduit between the candidate and the discipline.

What are the personal and professional benefits of research supervision?

Firstly, I gain immense personal pleasure from building relationships over a long period of time with capable and motivated students. Over the duration of a doctorate in particular, you come to know your students as individuals and emerging scholars far more than you can in large class context. As you come to know them you can tailor your supervision approach to what works best for them—some need regular deadlines; others need a lighter hand. You can also find opportunities for them to present at departmental seminars, attend conferences or contribute to publications.

"Ask your students what they envision for their future early on in the relationship—it may not be academia. Then connect them to a broad range of opportunities and resources that will assist them to get there."
(KD, early career academic)

Secondly, there are professional benefits from research supervision:
- You get an insight into a more detailed aspect of your wider field.
- The student's literature review brings you up-to-date with current research and thinking.
- You get to discuss theoretical and methodological ideas in depth with your co-supervisor and student.
- You gain confidence in your own knowledge of your discipline as you explain ideas and suggest readings.
- Supervisions contribute to and add variety to your workload.
- You are demonstrating that you are providing mentoring to emerging scholars and service to your discipline.
- You might find collaborative endeavours you can engage in with your student, such as presenting a symposium or co-publishing.
- You can nominate your students for appropriate awards, which also reflects to some extent on how well you have supervised or mentored them.

What is expected of you as a supervisor?

You will probably begin your career as a research supervisor by supporting an experienced supervisor with smaller projects, such as honours or masters dissertations. You might then take on your own masters supervisions and/or be invited to co-supervise doctoral theses. When you have gained enough experience in doctoral supervision you can become a lead supervisor. Each institution will have a set of expectations for supervision. You may be required to attend information seminars or undergo training before you can begin. There will probably be a website or booklets that you can access with all the policies and procedures you need to be aware of.

"Most institutions have some kind of guidelines for supervision that spell out the responsibilities of supervisors and student—and it's worth having a look at these and discussing them with your supervisors. Generally, most people argue that having good supervision makes a big difference to students' experience of undertaking doctoral research. Our research supports this, but it also shows that 'good supervision' means different things to different students and supervisors." (He Rautaki mo te Akoranga Kairangi)

Supervisions will be factored into your workload by being allocated hours or workload points. For a shared doctoral supervision, our faculty allocates 50 hours per supervisor per year. That is approximately one hour per week. About half of that time will be supervision meeting time and the other half will be reading students' work, preparing feedback, assisting with their ethical application, supporting candidates to present their proposal or helping them publish. I tell my students that this equates to us meeting face-to-face (or by Skype if either of us is off-site) 2 hours per month divided up in a way that suits us both. Most students choose an hour per fortnight but it depends where they are in the research process. Check the expectations at your institution.

With my co-supervisor, I like to discuss how we can build on each other's strengths and negotiate the division of workload. In some relationships, I might be the content expert and my co-supervisor the methodological expert; in other relationships it might be the other way round or a quite different combination. I really enjoy the big-picture thinking related to a thesis—how the theoretical framework and methodology complement each other or what conceptual themes are revealed by qualitative analysis. My supervision meetings usually involve sweeping diagrams on the whiteboard. I have other colleagues who like to focus on the details, such as writing style, argument logic, data display and accurate referencing. It is important to discuss how you best can work together to support the candidate.

The other relationship you have to negotiate is with the student. If you are the sole supervisor of a masters student or the lead supervisor of a doctoral candidate then it is up to you to set up the supervisory relationships with appropriate expectations. Here is an introductory discussion paper you might like to adapt and use at one of your first supervision meetings:

What we (the supervisors) can expect	What you (the candidate) can expect
• That you are willing to build a sound working relationship with your supervisors based on mutual respect and commitment	• That our supervisory relationship is based on everyone being committed to providing the expertise, advice and support you need to meet the exacting standards of a doctoral degree
• That you come prepared to engage in open discussion and be willing to accept advice and follow suggestions (within reason)	• That our relationship will be more formal to begin with as we set expectations and routines and form a working relationship
• That you will take responsibility for meeting any of the institution's requirements (such as English language competency, academic integrity modules or induction workshops)	• That at least one of the supervisors will be available for regular meetings as per the schedule we negotiate.
• That you will take responsibility for organising the supervision meetings (e.g., negotiating the time and sending calendar invites) and notify us well ahead of time if you need to reschedule	• That we will read work that has been provided to us at least a week ahead of time and give feedback as appropriate. Sometimes this will be verbal; sometimes written.
• That you will keep brief minutes of what was discussed and agreed and circulate after the meeting	• That we will provide readings, devise tasks, offer advice, require revisions and make deadlines and expect you to attend to these unless we negotiate otherwise
• That you will send any work that you want written feedback on at least a week ahead of time	• That we will support you through the provisional year requirements and help you devise a timeline to meet your completion date
• That you will send a brief agenda of items to be discussed at least 3 days ahead of time to give us time to prepare	• That we will find presentation opportunities (seminars, conferences or symposia) to allow you to share your ideas more widely
• That you keep us informed of what you are thinking, any changes of approach, new ideas or lines of interest so we are not taken by surprise	• That we will assist with publication opportunities, as appropriate, during and/or after your candidature
• That you will ultimately take responsibility for your learning, your research, the production of your thesis and the defence of your ideas	• That we will assist you to network with other candidates or colleagues where it will benefit your study
• That you will keep us informed of any matters that might hinder your progress	• That we will assist you to prepare for thesis submission and oral examination
• That you will raise issues of concern in an appropriate manner, as they arise	• That we will raise concerns that we have before they become big issues
• That if you feel the relationship has broken down you can ask for support from outside or to move to another supervisory relationship with no hard feelings	• That if we feel the relationship has broken down we will assist you to access support or find an alternative, such as a new supervisory relationship, with no hard feelings

How do you work with students whose backgrounds are different to your own?

While I have set out some introductory discussions to have with students in the table above—those ideas suit my very Pākehā ways of working. Many of my students come from ethnic and linguistic backgrounds different to my own—Māori, Pacific, Chinese, Indian, Nepalese, Colombian, Japanese, Chilean, Singaporean or Nigerian. They also represent different genders, sexual identities, abilities/disabilities, socio-economic backgrounds and personalities. One of the joys is that I come to know them and their understandings of the world in a way that enriches my own. These differences can be slightly uncomfortable at first as we begin to navigate our way through 'talking past each other.' They might also lead to tension where one of us acts in a way that mystifies or frustrates the other. Some suggestions that might help:

> "When Joan Metge wrote of traditional ako that 'learning is a very personal process in which the affection, respect, awe, maybe even love-hate relationship, between learner and "teacher" play a key part' (1983, p. 14), she could have been writing about doctoral supervision. It, too, is a very personal process in which emotional, sometimes even conflictual, elements can play a part. This does not necessarily mean the supervision is failing, although you need to find ways to cope with these emotions and still keep going." (He Rautaki mo te Akoranga Kairangi)

- Take the time find out more about how the student understands the relationship and their expectations so you can negotiate what will work for both of you.
- Set up the kind of relationship or meeting structure that allows issues to be freely but respectfully raised (that is one of the reasons I ask for the student to set the agenda so they have an opportunity to raise anything of concern).
- Include cultural, linguistic, content or other advisors as part of the supervision team or point your student in the right direction for networks or support.
- Become familiar with research and ethical guidelines that support you to work with students from different cultures and in different cultural contexts when undertaking research.
- Improve your own knowledge of diversity (for example, learn te reo, attend a diversity workshop or get advice from your LGBTQ colleagues).

- Assist the student to find opportunities to improve their English language or academic writing, if that is an issue.
- With some international students you might need to explain that using first names and informal language and behaviour does not imply that the relationship is any less serious or expectations any less rigorous.
- Explain the way the New Zealand doctoral system works if it is different from their own.
- Find a balance that suits you both when supporting the pastoral care side of the relationship.

What do you do when issues arise?

Unfortunately issues do arise and relationships, despite everyone's best efforts, can break down. This is why I raise the possibility early on so both parties know that they can leave the relationship with dignity. Because the relationship is intense and might have gone on for a long time, the breakdown can still be distressing for both parties. If you have tried your best to resolve these issues within the supervision team and this has not worked then it is time to go beyond the research relationship. There will be support systems for both parties through the doctoral adviser, postgraduate office, students' association or counselling service. The relationship might require mediation through a third party. If, finally, it cannot be resolved then I find it is better to assist the student to make a clear decision to move on—this might be to find new supervisors, to take leave, to exit the programme or change institutions. I tell my students that I have their best interests at heart and sometimes this might mean making hard decisions or having difficult conversations. If you have concerns about a more serious offence, such as deliberate plagiarism, it is important that you get your doctoral adviser or postgraduate office involved as soon as possible as these are matters you cannot resolve yourself.

These matters are rare. In my supervision of over 40 postgraduate students, I have had one case of serious plagiarism, one student counselled out of doctoral study, one student moved to another supervisor and several students take periods of prolonged leave. With the others, we have covered the gamut of emotions but, in the end, we have survived with the relationship intact and the student successfully completing their studies.

What is involved in examining theses and dissertations?

Examining theses and dissertations (and the use of these terms varies across institutions) is part of the expectation of being an academic. You are doing your part in assessing the credibility of new research in your field.

Early in my career I found that examining theses and sitting on examination committees made me a better writer and a better supervisor. Having a wider range of examples—good and bad—gave me benchmarks against which to measure my own work and the work of my students. Becoming more familiar with thesis expectations through having to write to the thesis examination criteria and being part of discussions where we reviewed examiners' reports and finalised thesis grades helped me focus in on what really matters.

Thesis reports can vary from institution to institution. Some ask you to write to specified headings; others ask for a narrative that covers key points. Some ask for a specific mark or grade; others ask for the thesis to be placed in a grade range. Some ask you to annotate corrections on the hard copy; others ask you to note the expected corrections in the report. There is a difference in expectation between honours dissertations, masters theses and doctoral theses. There might also be different expectations across disciplines or types of degrees, however, there are generally similar expectations:

- Does the thesis show that the candidate has a sound knowledge of the field and the relevant bodies of literature? Is the literature and/or prior research appropriately acknowledged? Are the referencing conventions followed?

- Does the thesis meet the conventions of the discipline? This can vary markedly from the hard sciences, to a conceptual or philosophical thesis or a performance degree, so you need to be familiar with what the different expectations are.

- If it is an empirical thesis, does it adequately detail the question, methods, analysis and interpretation? Does the study appear to be soundly implemented?

- If it is a more philosophical or discursive thesis, does it have a logic and coherence consistent with its field?

- Is it grounded within a clearly explained paradigm, theoretical or conceptual framework?
- Were ethical considerations covered adequately?
- Do the findings contribute new knowledge or make an original contribution to the field?
- Is it well-written, well-presented, well-argued, clearly laid out and error free?

I usually take a four-stage approach to examining a thesis. First, I read the abstract, introduction and conclusion. I might then skim read chapter introductions or summaries. I'm trying to get a feel for what the candidate was trying to do, how they did it and what they achieved. Second, I set aside time to read sections more thoroughly. If I have a hard copy, I annotate in pencil as I go. If I have an electronic copy, I'll make sticky note comments. Third, I'll read all my comments and pull them together under headings, either ones that are supplied or that I create. By this stage, I will have a good idea of what grade range or examination category this thesis sits in. Fourth, I write my report, drawing on my annotations, my summary and my reflections. My reports usually follow this pattern:

- A general introduction: *'In this thesis the candidate investigated …'*
- Strengths: *"I would like to commend the candidate's use of …"*
- Areas for consideration: *"The thesis could have been strengthened if …"*
- Criteria—as outlined in that institution's guidelines (literature, methodology, etc.).
- Overall comment—a more general statement that gives my judgement of the quality of the thesis.
- Grade as requested (often on a separate sheet from the report).
- Corrections—these might range from typos to be corrected before the thesis is placed in the library to asking for sections to be revised before the degree can be granted.

As I have examined (and supervised) more theses at different levels, I have honed my skills but I have also become more aware of time, word length and other limitations. My advice from this experience is:

- Make sure you examine the thesis as presented—not the one that you would have written.

- Take into account the time or word length restrictions. You can't expect a 20,000-word dissertation completed in 6 months to have the depth of a much longer one.
- While you should not excuse bad grammar and punctuation or poor proofreading, be aware that there are many different styles of writing. These vary across disciplines and modern usage of English is less pedantic than it has been. Students for whom English is not their first language might also have different ways of expressing ideas than native English speakers. I find that on my second or third read through I have adjusted to the writer's style and I focus more on the ideas than the expression.
- Within the bounds of confidentiality you can seek advice from your mentor or an experienced colleague if you are unsure of how to deal with something that arises as you examine a thesis. This is especially important if you suspect plagiarism.

Finally, enjoy the process. Yes, there will be a few theses that are hard to read and write about but many are a good read. I find that I often gain new insights into topics I'm interested in and there are references they have used that I might follow up. A really good thesis can be a good as reading a novel. It draws you in and you want to read right to the end. These make the effort worthwhile.

Chapter 12 Engaging in service

He aha te mea nui o te ao

He tangata, he tangata, he tangata

What is the most important thing in the world?

It is people, it is people, it is people

- What is service?
- How do you contribute at a collegial level?
- What is expected at departmental or institutional level?
- What can you do in the service of your discipline?
- How do you offer service to your profession?
- How can you engage in community service?

I have heard that beginning academics have been told to avoid service and focus on their research if they want to get ahead. I find this advice problematic. Academic organisations, such as universities and polytechnics, function through a layered committee structure, which aims to gain input from staff at all levels of the institution. Proposing a new programme might begin at a departmental committee level, progressing through faculty-wide panels and community consultation on to university-wide panels and in New Zealand, to national bodies. In order for such a system to offer opportunities for a range of voices to be heard and sensible decisions to be made we need to have academics sitting on these committees.

University and community service contributions are expected and an academic's salary and workload recognises this expectation. Once I have encouraged new staff members to participate on school, faculty or university-wide committees or working parties, they find that they have their own rewards—networking with a wider group of people, gaining a better understanding of how the organisation works, and having an opportunity to contribute to important decision-making.

> "Engage in service activities. I was often advised against it, instead being told to focus on research and writing. I found my service activities to be engaging, a great way to connect with colleagues across the Faculty, and helped confirm what kind of academic I wish to be." (JT, early career academic)

What is service?

As I have indicated, service is part of an academic's workload. At my institution, workloads are generally divided into 40% teaching (including supervision), 40% research, and 20% service. At a minimum, service is attending relevant meetings related to the units (schools, centres, departments, faculties) you are attached to. You are also expected to sit on committees, working parties and panels. These might be committees that deal with academic matters, such as Boards of Studies, examination committees or programme committees. They might relate to the wider life of the organisation, such as equity, library, IT or social committees. Outside the organisation, you are also expected to contribute to your discipline and/or profession through such activities as professional associations, editorial boards or conference committees. Many people also give their time and expertise to their communities through union, cultural, research, and charitable or other activities. In short, service is giving back to the organisation and the units within it and recognising the privilege afforded to you as an academic and seeking ways to use your expertise to enrich the lives of others. Meeting more that the minimum service expectations is usually a requirement for continuation and promotion. My best advice is to find service opportunities that will hold your interest and not feel like a chore. You might even find that service leads to management and leadership experiences that add interest to your work and valuable career opportunities.

How do you contribute at a collegial level?

In order to create a welcoming and supportive work environment we all need to play a part in creating a culture of collegiality. While you might feel that as a new member of staff, you don't have much to offer, a friendly greeting, a conversation opening, a book to share or taking your turn to clear away the cups can be more important to your academic and general staff colleagues than all the amazing findings in your research. Remember too, that people helped you along the way so there might be ways you can reciprocate—taking a class when someone is ill, offering to help with marking or making doctoral candidates or new staff welcome. As Maya Angelou said, "I've learned that people will forget what you said, people will forget what you did, but people will never forget how you made them feel."

"Don't be afraid to offer your ideas. Have faith in the idea that you have something valuable to contribute (even if sometimes you feel awkward)." (CC, early career academic).

What is expected at a departmental or institutional level?

Your departmental head or mentor might recommend service opportunities for you. Look around and see where your interest or expertise might sit well. Are there policies or procedures you don't agree with—maybe you can make a difference by joining the committee that administers those policies or the working party that is reviewing them. In our institution, service is 20% of an academic's workload—that is a full day per week. I am always surprised when colleagues say they have no time for service. What are they doing on that day a week when they are paid to make service contributions to their institution, discipline and community?

One of the key service expectations is attending meetings. On this point, I'd like to outline my expectations for meeting etiquette. You can contribute to efficient and effective meetings by:

- Reading or at least scanning the agenda and documents ahead of time.
- Arriving on time or notifying the chair you might be late. This is especially important if a quorum is required.
- Turning up or putting in an apology.
- Keeping your comments clear, brief and to the point.

- Providing a written paper ahead of time if you have an important matter to raise.
- Keeping personal conversations and the checking of your electronic devices to a minimum and unobtrusive.
- Not using meetings to promote personal agendas.
- Thanking the chair—you'll appreciate their efforts once you start chairing meetings yourself.
- Taking your turn—to take minutes, set up the room, clear away the cups or whatever tasks might need to be done.

As you begin to move up the career ladder you will be expected to become more involved in matters beyond your work-related units. These are often the most rewarding committees, working parties or panels to be part of. You get to know people from a range of other fields and to see the variety of teaching and scholarship that goes on at your institution.

"Look for service opportunities that you believe in and put your name forward before you are assigned something less interesting so that you can make an authentic and meaningful contribution as an academic citizen." (KD, early career academic)

At this level you often see the fruits of your committee labours more quickly. You can exert more influence over an outcome and see immediate results. As people across the wider institution get to know you, they might keep you in mind for other inter-departmental or cross-disciplinary opportunities.

What can you do in the service of your discipline?

Just as institutions rely on voluntary labour to staff committees and contribute to decision-making, so do your disciplinary or professional bodies. When everyone who belongs to an organisation takes their turn filling roles on the executive committee, editorial board or conference committee, it eases the burden on all and promotes diversity and inclusiveness.

"A community of scholarship depends on generosity of spirit and your willingness to give back." (PO, senior academic)

A young colleague asked how she might get known in her discipline. I noticed that a new journal had started up in her field and I suggested she write in outlining her wide experience in the field and offer to sit on the editorial board or act as a reviewer. To her delight she was accepted on to the editorial board and asked to submit an article for their next issue.

Ways you could consider contributing to your discipline:
- Attend annual general meetings to get to know the organisation and people.
- Offer to take up roles within the organisation. You can always start by helping out with the annual conference.
- Consider setting up a special interest group.
- Offer to review for journals in your field. Send the editor your CV and an example of your published work if you do not already know them.
- Offer to mentor or run workshops for the student members of the organisation. They often welcome hearing from someone who is not too far up the food chain.
- Contribute to the organisation's newsletter by writing short pieces or book reviews.
- Let your mentor or senior colleagues know that you are ready to give more time to your association. You might end up being nominated to the executive committee.

How do you offer service to your profession?

Not all academic disciplines are tied to professions but there are many that are—education, nursing, law, engineering, accounting, medicine and social work to name a few. Many academics in these fields come from the profession and may have had many years as a practitioner. They may still retain their professional accreditation and be engaged in the accrediting body or professional society. If this is the field you come from or are working towards, there are several ways that you can contribute to service through your profession.

Firstly, if you meet the criteria you can be involved in practice clinics or visiting students undertaking practical experiences in the relevant workplace. In my faculty we train teachers, social workers and counsellors. Each of these programmes requires lecturers with knowledge or experience of the profession. In teaching, the Education Council expects that pre-service teachers spend a certain proportion of their training in schools or early childhood centres gaining practical experience. Visiting these students on their placements is not only part of the role of many of our lecturers, it a service to the profession. It ensures that the next generation of professionals gets current experience and that the lecturers who teach them are regularly in the professional context and interacting with practising teachers and principals. The social work disciplinary body also expects that everyone who teaches into their preparation programmes still maintains current professional accreditation. See the work that you do in preparing the new professionals in your field as a service to your department, faculty, profession and the wider community. This way it is not a chore but a privilege.

Secondly, you can engage with your profession outside of your institutional context. Your location in a tertiary institution that provides training for the profession gives you credibility and status. Use this this to give back to the profession by taking a role on a committee or regulatory body or by volunteering to run professional development, speak at seminars or assist with conferences. If your profession has a journal, you can write for that or offer to review or sit on the editorial board.

Thirdly, you can be a conduit between your profession and the courses you teach. Are there opportunities to bring practitioners in to speak to your students, contribute to programme development or sit on an advisory group? It is important that we are not seen as sitting in our ivory towers divorced from our colleagues in the profession.

How can you engage in community service?

For many Māori and Pacific academics community service is a way of life. As their status increases in their workplace, it often also increases in their community and this calls for an enormous commitment of time. For those of us without such expectations from our community, it is helpful to our Māori and Pasifika colleagues to understand the many and diverse roles they need to play and the time required to meet all their community requests. If you do not belong to a community that has these calls on your time, there are still ways that you can use your expertise to support your wider community. Amongst my colleagues I know people who are involved with refugees and new migrants, prisoners and families of prisoners, adult literacy, oral history, environmental issues, sports coaching, school boards of trustees, community boards, youth at risk and political or educational lobby groups. There is no compulsion to be part of your wider community and your circumstances might limit the time you have available. My feeling is that it keeps your feet on the ground and the expertise you can offer might really make a difference.

Chapter 13 Seminars and conferences

Ko te pae tawhiti whāia kia tata, ko te pae tata whakamaua kia tina

Seek out distant horizons, and cherish those you attain

- Why is attending and participating in seminars important?
- What can you gain from attending and presenting at conferences?
- How do you give professional presentations?
- How do you engage in networking and follow up?
- Should you publish in conference proceedings?

Why is attending and participating in seminars important?

As your role as an academic is to contribute to your field and to society's knowledge base as a whole, it is important that you get your work out there to be shared with and scrutinised by your peers.

Part of your contribution to the life of your centre, department or faculty is to support your colleagues by attending their research seminars where you can and by presenting aspects of your work at seminars and symposia within and across the institution.

Many departments have lunchtime seminar series. It is a great opportunity to get to know your colleagues and their work. Visiting scholars are also asked to present seminars, workshops and lectures. This is an opportunity to gain an overview of their key ideas or catch up with their latest research. Institutions often have formal lecture series inviting top national or international guests. As a Visiting Fellow at the London School of Economics in 2014, I could have filled my day with so many interesting lectures that I needed to become a little more selective in order to make best use of my time.

You might have already presented a departmental seminar as part of your doctoral requirements. Many people who attended that seminar would be keen to know how your study turned out and what direction you are now taking your research. Don't be shy. The staff member responsible for putting a seminar series together will be very pleased to hear from you. It is also a good opportunity to meet people from your wider department or faculty with complementary interests. Don't just focus on opportunities that are already there but think about how you can fill a gap by arranging your own seminar series or using your networks to invite a speaker to your faculty.

What can you gain from attending and presenting at conferences?

As a doctoral candidate or early career academic you can be overwhelmed by the range of conferences on offer. Conferences are a great place to outline your ideas to an audience of peers and to network with like-minded people. Conferences can range from smaller, focused local or national annual meetings to huge multi-disciplinary conferences taking up numerous hotel and conference facilities in a major international city.

"Go to conferences you are interested in. Sometimes it's good to try something new. I had a wonderful time presenting at the Philosophy of Education conference. It was outside my usual cohort but a great chance to learn and think." (CC, early career academic).

I suggest, that unless you go with a group of colleagues who can show you the ropes, that you start small. A conference of 50–100 people means you are more likely to get an audience. You will get to see the same people over the conference duration and therefore it is easier to start up a conversation and to meet more than once. While a large refereed conference might look better on your CV, you might find it a lonelier, less engaging experience. Often as a first time speaker at an international conference you might find yourself in a bare room with an audience of two or sitting by yourself at a roundtable presentation. Going to a national association or smaller disciplinary conference, especially if you already know a few attendees, might be a better place to start.

You also need to be aware that you will receive email invitations to conferences that are held in exotic locations and cover a huge list of topics. These are usually put together for moneymaking rather than intellectual purposes and are best avoided. If unsure, talk to you mentor or other colleagues.

If you are not sure which format to select when you submit your proposal, here is a summary of advantages and disadvantages:

Type	Description	Advantages	Disadvantages
Poster	Your poster is put on display and you stand beside it at allotted times to engage passers-by in discussion.	These are not always peer-reviewed so often have a higher acceptance rate for new academics. You have discussions with people genuinely interested in your topic.	You can do a lot of standing and waiting. Posters are not considered as highly on your list of outputs.
Roundtable	You sit at a table by yourself or with several other presenters with papers on the same topic. You each do a short presentation then those around your table discuss the papers presented.	You are allotted a longer period of time. You get to meet others with similar interests. You get to discuss your papers and others' papers in more depth. A full paper is not usually expected.	You might not attract an audience as many roundtables are scheduled at the same time. You are often your own chair and timekeeper.
Paper	You present a summarised version of a completed paper as part of a session of linked papers. You are allotted presentation and question time. This can vary from 10–30 minutes.	These generally attract larger audiences. You get to hear other work on a similar topic and meet presenters working in your field. Someone chairs and keeps time.	You might be only allocated 10 minutes to present and it can be hard to reduce your paper to the time limit. People come and go between papers and this can be disconcerting.
Symposium	You are invited to present your paper as part of a linked set of papers on a topic. Your symposium is often allocated a double slot so you have more time.	Symposia attract audiences who are very interested in the topic and the different perspectives presented. Discussion is often in more depth and lively.	Symposia take up more space on a conference programme, so not many sessions are allocated. You need to be invited or you need to arrange colleagues to participate.

Panel	You are invited to present your views on a particular topic along with others. The idea is to engage the audience in discussion. You do not usually have a full paper prepared.	These are often more prestigious as you are invited because you have expertise in an aspect of the topic. You get exposure as someone respected in the field.	You can never predict the way the questions or discussion will go. The audience may not follow up on your area or they might ask questions out of left field.
Workshop	A workshop is usually a longer session with a practical focus. Participants expect it to be more hands-on and to have materials provided.	You get a chance to share a practical application of your work. Your audience is interested in learning how they can apply your ideas themselves.	It takes much more preparation. It is more intensive. It takes up more time on the conference programme.

If you are invited to a large conference to present a paper, talk on a panel, as part of a symposium or to attend with a group of colleagues, don't shy away from the opportunity. Here are a few tips:

- Browse the on-line programme ahead of time to get a sense of how this conference operates.
- It is better to follow a theme or SIG (Special Interest Group) than to try to spread yourself across too many topics.
- Take advantage of emerging scholar, international guest, special interest group or alumni social events to get to know people.
- Take the opportunity to ask a question or offer a comment in a session as this might resonate with other audience members.
- Take your business cards and distribute liberally (but don't necessarily expect to get them in return).
- Take the opportunity to introduce yourself to people you admire or who captured your interest (but don't overstay your welcome).
- Attend the trade shows or exhibits to view new ideas or publications; take advantage of discounts offered (but get the goods sent to you rather than try to take a suitcase full of heavy material home).
- Travel light. While you need one smart outfit for your presentation day or conference dinner most of the time you can be dressy casual (however, check that your dress is culturally and professionally appropriate for the context).

How do you give a professional presentation?

Timing is everything. Whether your discipline expects you to read a prepared paper or use a PowerPoint summary, no one, yourself included, enjoys a paper that is presented too quickly or runs out of time. Practice at home or with a critical friend. Have a dry run at a departmental seminar to get your timing right. It is important that you practice out loud—it is not the same when you say it inside your head.

Think about your audience. Unless it is a methodological conference, they will be most interested in your findings. They can always read your paper to get the finer details of research design and context. Your audience will appreciate clearly delivered, logically structured memorable key points rather than endless detail. Don't try to tell them everything you did or found—choose a few take-away messages that you introduce and elaborate with useful examples.

If you are using PowerPoint, use it sparingly. Each slide should be a brief summary or image that is your prompt to expand upon. The audience should be focused on what you say rather than what's on the screen. If you are going to use tables or diagrams, simplify them so they can be easily viewed from the back of the room. The following table shows how you could structure a 15-minute presentation. You will see that you don't get much time at all.

Structuring a conference presentation		
• Title slide, presenter's name and institution, conference location	1 slide	30 seconds
• Introduction/mihi		30 seconds
• Presentation outline	1 slide	30 seconds
• Topic, question, key literature	2 slides	2 minutes
• Research design overview	2 slides	3 minutes
• Selected findings	3 slides	5 minutes
• Discussion and implications	2 slides	3 minutes
• Closing Adapted from: Mutch, C. (2013). *Doing Educational Research*, p. 183	1 slide	30 seconds

How do you engage in networking and follow up?

One of the key reasons for going to conferences, after getting yourself and your research better known, is to network with people with similar interests. When I first started working in disaster research, I would go to conferences where I knew nobody. Talking to people who came to my presentation or to presenters after their sessions was invaluable. These conversations led to joint research projects, co-authoring, grant writing and even setting up our own international network of researchers interested in children's experiences of disasters.

"The most rewarding thing I did: My research got picked up by a small research group in Canada after some of their members attended a conference presentation I gave. Later that year, I Skyped in to one of their meetings and we discussed two of my articles, which they had read in preparation. I was thrilled for my doctoral research to have reached exactly the people it was written for."
(MM, early career academic)

A young colleague asked me what she should do with the business cards and e-mail addresses she had collected at a large international conference. Was she expected to make contact with the people she had met? I responded that these relationships often take time to develop as people get to meet each other again over subsequent years. In fact, many lasting collaborations and friendships can come from regularly meeting up at the same conferences year after year. My advice to her was to pick one or two that she thought might have potential and drop them a quick line, possibly sending one of her articles that might be of interest. There might never be a reply but that was not a sign that next time they met she would have been forgotten. As academics return to their busy lives, other priorities take over. I find I don't follow up until something comes up, which I think might be of interest to that person or of mutual benefit. As an editor I have contacted young academics post-conference inviting them to submit to a special issue or edited book—so these opportunities might also come your way.

Should you publish in conference proceedings?

A frequently asked question is whether to have your paper published in the conference proceedings. The answer depends on what is appropriate for your discipline. In some fields, especially in the sciences, conference proceedings are blind peer-reviewed and considered prestigious. In other fields, you are better to publish in a reputable journal. Ask your disciplinary colleagues what is best for you. It is not good form to have your paper appear in conference proceedings and then be published again in another format unchanged (see the section in Chapter 9 on self-plagiarism). Any subsequent version should be significantly revised and have a different title to avoid confusion or misunderstanding.

Chapter 14 Preparing for continuation and promotion

Ehara taku toa, he takitahi, he toa takitini

My success should not be bestowed on me alone, as it was not individual success but success of a collective

- How do you make the most of your time prior to tenure?
- How do you prepare for confirmation or continuation?
- How do you build an evidence portfolio?
- How are different cultural approaches taken into consideration?
- What do you need to do to be ready for promotion?

How do you make the most of your time prior to tenure?

Many new academics start with part-time and/or short-term contracts. While the tentative nature of this employment might seem unsettling, it is nevertheless a good opportunity to hone your teaching skills, put your research into practice and get some publications underway. It is also a really useful opportunity to learn from those around you. Observe how your department or faculty operates. Become familiar with policies and practices. Attend research seminars and professional development workshops. Ask to sit in on classes and tutorials. It is also an important time for you to demonstrate your areas of interest and expertise. Offer to sit on committees and working groups. Share your research in a departmental seminar.

Get known as someone who is prepared to do their bit. Don't be the person who always complains that the coffee machine is empty. It's the little things that are noticed and remembered when opportunities arise. When a job vacancy is advertised you will have a better sense of what the department expects and you will have new experiences to add to your CV (see Chapter 2).

Once you have secured a permanent or tenured position there might still be a period of probation before your appointment is confirmed. This is important for both you and your department to see if you are a good fit. You might be expected to attend induction seminars or professional development workshops. Don't be precious about these. Experienced academics arriving at a new institution are often expected to attend these as well. It's as much about being acculturated into the new institution's expectations and ways of doing things as it is about gaining information.

> *"The most rewarding thing I did: Returning the favour of finding great colleagues and mentors by being generous with my time. This included helping out colleagues, showing appreciation for our administrative staff, and going out of my way to be welcoming to our postgraduate students."* (JT, early career academic).

You might also be assigned a buddy or mentor. A buddy helps you settle in and answers those awkward questions you are shy about asking others. A mentor helps you focus on developing career goals and strategies (see Chapter 5). Use these people wisely—tap into their knowledge and experience without taking up too much of their time.

> *"The most helpful thing I did: I found several wonderful mentors."* (JT, early career academic).

Your institution will have regular, probably annual, performance appraisal or academic development meetings between staff members and their line managers. See this as a helpful experience to collate your achievements in one place. As you look over the past year, you will be surprised how much you have completed in relation to teaching, research and service. You might also notice gaps or tasks that you didn't get to. You now have the opportunity to use your annual review to reconsider your future plans. Your academic head, line manager or mentor can help you design achievable short-term goals that build towards the completion of your longer-term plans (see also Chapter 5 on how to best use your mentor).

How do you prepare for confirmation or continuation?

After a time, you might be expected to apply for confirmation or meet continuation criteria. The most useful advice that I can offer is to know your job expectations well and record the activities (with supporting evidence) that you have undertaken to meet these requirements to the expected standard. Here are some examples:

Expectation	Examples	Evidence of quality
Will undertake high quality teaching that is responsive to student feedback	Course director EDUC 123, *Introduction to Educational Thought* Lecturer on BIO 760 Tutor for BUS 204 & 304	* Formal student evaluation 86% satisfaction rating. Adapted tutorial after student feedback. * Invited by Prof Briggs to present doctoral research to postgraduate course * *"Thanks so much for your clear and helpful explanations"* (student evaluation, BUS 204)
Will demonstrate commitment to the Treaty of Waitangi	Attended introductory te reo course. Included readings with Māori perspective in EDUC 123	* Achieved basic fluency in mihi and conversational phrases * *"The Mason Durie reading was useful in helping our understanding"* (student evaluation EDUC 123)
Will achieve two peer-reviewed outputs per year	Mills, S. (2016). Academia in the post-truth era. *Journal of Higher Education*. Mills, S. (2016). From novice to expert. *Journal of Performative Pedagogy*.	* Journal Impact Factor: 0.875 * Invited to contribute to special issue by journal editor
Will contribute to departmental planning and decision-making as required	School representative on Faculty Equity Committee Working party to review undergraduate programmes	* Attended monthly meetings and reported back to school * Attended four meetings and contributed to draft working paper

How do you prepare your evidence portfolio?

When it comes to preparing your application and completing the required forms you will be expected to provide evidence to support your claims. This will include quantitative data (for example, number of courses, number of students in a course, satisfaction ratings, journal impact factors or citation rates). It will also require independent verification of the quality of your teaching or impact of your service. Here are some suggestions to start your data gathering.

Quantitative data

- Become familiar with your institution's systems for generating course-related or timetable data. These could include course numbers, hours you were assigned to teach in a course, pass rates, grade distributions and retention rates.
- Go through your diary (electronic or hard copy) to record how many meetings you attended of your committees or working parties and to work out how many hours a task, such as writing a position paper, might have taken.
- Check your emails to record numbers of invitations to contribute to other courses, speak at seminars, join a supervision team or review for a journal.
- Encourage your students to complete course evaluations of your teaching. Anonymous or independently verified evaluations add a measure of credibility to the claims you are making. I acknowledge there can be flaws or anomalies with such processes but at best they can show trends over time and across different courses.

Qualitative data

- Include open-ended questions in your student evaluations to get an insight into what you do well and what could be improved.
- Show how you have taken feedback on board and modified your lectures or assessments.
- Ask a respected colleague or someone from your institution's teaching and learning committee or centre to observe your teaching and provide independent feedback. You can also ask them to conduct a survey of students you supervise.

It really helps if you update the record of your activities regularly. When I have done this I'm always surprised by how much I had forgotten. Perhaps set aside time each month to collate and record your activities and to file examples of supporting evidence. This will save you time when you need to complete applications for continuation or promotion in a short timeframe.

Think about innovative ways in which you can gather data. You can take screen shots of any digital material you have posted. You can take photographs of wall displays, whiteboard discussions, student activities or field trips. Similarly you can make audio or video recordings (with permission) of class discussions, presentations or of your own teaching or reflections on your teaching.

> *"The least helpful thing I did: Initially trying to emulate others. I wasn't successful until I stopped trying to become another version of someone else and instead focused on finding my own niche."* (JT, early career academic)

What is the place of your teaching portfolio?

In Chapter 6 we discussed setting up a teaching portfolio. As you gain more teaching experience, you need to keep updating this. Ako Aotearoa offer advice for preparing portfolios for their teaching awards. While you might not feel ready for such awards, this advice might help you with your continuation or promotion applications. They suggest that:

- You put your students and the quality of their learning experiences at the heart of your teaching portfolio.
- You outline your personal values and beliefs and where these influences have come from.
- You display your knowledge and understanding of learners and the learning process.
- You discuss your idea of the optimum teaching and learning environment and your views of the inter-relationship between teaching and learning.
- You show understanding of both discipline-specific and generic learning outcomes.
- You collect evidence of an ongoing commitment to learning more about teaching and improving your own teaching.
- You engage in leadership relative to your level and context.

How are different cultural approaches taken into consideration?

I would like to say that different cultural values and perspectives are always given serious consideration but, unfortunately, this is not always the case. This is where it is really important to get support from your cultural networks and mentors. There are precedents in some fields and institutions where non-Western approaches are the norm but it will require you to seek these out and use them as evidence to support the case you are making. It will take courage to challenge conventions but it is important that these issues are raised. Here is an example from Ako Aotearoa where the teaching awards recognise a kaupapa Māori approach to teaching. Ako Aotearoa's website also provides an example of a winning portfolio using the following criteria. While you might not feel ready for such recognition, use the criteria to structure portfolios that are needed for other aspects of your academic life such as your teaching portfolio or a continuation application. Note, in Ako Aotearoa's example, the portfolio was compiled from interviews with the applicant, testimonies from colleagues and students, and evidence from other sources but submitted by his colleagues with "his reluctant consent and humility." The criteria used to make the award are summarised below:

Key criteria	Related concepts
Mana – Leadership and Professional Development	• Rangatiratanga – Leadership • Kaupapa Māori – Māori concepts • Mātauranga Māori – Māori knowledge • *Ūkaipōtanga* – Loyalty • Whānaungatanga – Relationships • Kaitiakitanga – Guardianship/sustainability
Whakaakoranga – Teaching Excellence – Design for Learning, Facilitating Learning	• Kairangi – Excellence • Pūkengatanga – Skills • Manaakitanga – Concern for colleagues and learners • Kotahitanga – Collaboration
Mātaki – Assessing Student Learning, Evaluation of Learning and Teaching	• *Ākonga* – Learners • Kaiako – Teaching • Taunaki – Evidence
Source: https://akoaotearoa.ac.nz/download/ng/file/group-4/procedures-guidelines-and-criteria---ttea-2017.pdf	

What do you need to do to be ready to apply for promotion?

Become familiar with your institution's criteria for promotion, especially those for the next steps in your career progression. If you have followed the advice in this book so far—used a mentor to help with career planning, kept accurate records of your achievements and maintained a research and publication plan—you will be well prepared for the task of applying for promotion.

If you have built up good relationships with your mentor and colleagues, they will be happy to look over your application and give you advice. Your HR team can assist you here as well. If you ask for advice, you need to be prepared for advice that might not be as pos-

> *"Don't do things just for promotion but because it needs to be done and you believe it needs to be done."* (PO, senior academic)

itive as you had hoped. You might not agree but you should always evaluate it to see if your timing is right or you are getting the balance, tone or level of detail right.

Be careful not to oversell or undersell your achievements. Be accurate. Don't bluff or exaggerate. The academic world, especially in New Zealand, is a small place. You never know who might sit on a panel or be asked to provide input. Having said that, as I noted above, there is a culture in New Zealand of downplaying achievements, especially between Māori and Pacific peoples, where it is inappropriate to laud your own success. If your institution does not have protocols for Māori and Pacific academics to ensure that they receive due recognition then those of us who are not from those cultures need to support our colleagues by speaking up. The whakataukī: *Kāore te kumara e kōrero mō tōna ake reka*, reminds us that the kumara doesn't say how sweet it is but we can all provide supportive evidence of our colleagues' value, contributions and achievements.

Prepare your application well in advance. Ensure you address the criteria. Provide verifiable evidence where required. Ask your mentor or a trusted colleague to review your application. Let your head of department or unit manager and referees know you are applying so that they can be prepared to complete their part of the process. Choose your referees carefully. Ensure they can talk about how you meet the criteria. It is helpful to ask them well ahead of time and provide them with the criteria and a copy of your application so they are able to respond appropriately. Complete all the sections. Proofread. Hand in on time.

If you are unsuccessful, use this as a learning opportunity. First, do your own reflection. Were you premature? Did you misunderstand the requirements? Second, ask for feedback. Why were you unsuccessful? What do you need to do to address the shortfall before you next apply? Third, put a plan in place with a realistic timeline to meet that criteria. Remember all the while to sustain the activities that address all the other criteria. Try not to dwell too much on the disappointment. Your academic career should be providing you with plenty of intrinsic rewards through your teaching, research and service so that promotion or non-promotion does not define who you are and why you do what you do. Hard to do, I know, but I have learned this from my own experiences. Respond with dignity. People will remember this more than whether you were successful or not.

Chapter 15 Disseminating your research more widely

Rurea, taitea, kia tū ko taikākā anake

Strip away the bark and expose the heartwood

- How do you increase your academic uptake?
- How do you spread your ideas more widely?
- How do you influence policy and practice?
- How do you engage with the media?
- How do you exercise your critic and conscience role?

If you want your research to be read and cited, your findings to influence policy or your ideas to make a difference in your field, then these things do not happen without conscious effort. You need to think in terms of your multiple audiences and the best ways to engage their interest in your work.

"Rewrite the rule book. If people are interested in what you have to share, share it." (CC, early career academic)

How do you increase your academic uptake?

Citations have become an important metric in measuring the impact of your work. There are a range of sites that that act as repositories of your work, connect you to a wide range of readership and gather data such as numbers of downloads or citations. Some sites, such as Scopus or Web of Science, give a journal's Impact Factor or SNIP (Source Normalized Impact per Paper). There are also sites that record how many times you appear in the media or how many libraries have purchased copies of your books. There are, of course, critics of bibliometrics because they tend to favour large publishing companies and well-established journals with wide circulation. However, it seems that promotions committees and PBRF panels take note of these metrics as indications of the quality and impact of your work. The sites best for you will vary across disciplines, for example, Web of Science for the hard sciences and Google Scholar for the arts and humanities. The best advice will come from your subject librarian.

Let's start with an article you have just had accepted. To make it more easily accessible by sites such as Google Scholar or ResearchGate, you need to check which version you are allowed to put on your personal website, in your institution's repository and/or upload to such sites. If you can't find the information in the publishing agreement or on the publisher's website, check with your librarian. You might also have been offered 50 free downloads of your article. You can either put the link at the bottom of your email signature or send the link to interested colleagues. Use this option promptly as there is often a time limit.

A publishing company might have also offered you other opportunities to increase your readership such as uploading a slide presentation or short video. I have never taken up the option of submitting a PowerPoint slide show, audio or video summary of work (mainly because of time pressures) but editors and publishers do report that it increases interest in your work. The publishers that offer this service provide helpful instructions to follow. It is certainly worth a try.

Once your article is published, the citation will be picked up by the various search engines already mentioned. If the article is open access, a reader can download from the link. Otherwise you will need to sign up to the site and upload the published article, pre-publication submission or an unpublished draft, according to the article publisher's restrictions, so that it can be accessed by interested readers. You will probably need to sign up to several of these sites as they have different ways of accessing your articles and different sites favour different publishers or journals. Different parts of the world also use some sites more than others, for example, Academia.edu rather than ResearchGate. What is helpful about such sites is that they gather metrics on how often your article is downloaded (e.g., Mendeley), read on-line (e.g.,

ResearchGate) or cited (e.g., Google Scholar). They also give you some kind of rating. Google Scholar, for example, gives you an h-index (the highest number of articles with a certain number of citations–that is, an h-index of 13 says that 13 of your articles have 13 or more citations). Google Scholar also provides an i10-index (how many of your articles are cited more than 10 times). Once you have signed up to these sites you will be notified of updates (new readers, requests for copies and so on). This can become intrusive and time consuming and you could even become overly obsessive about your ratings and scores. Such sites can provide helpful statistics for your CV or academic portfolio and some are useful for networking but unless you have lots of time at your disposal don't let them distract you too much.

How do you spread your ideas more widely?

There are other ways you can get your work noticed closer to home. Put links to the journal on your website or e-mail sign-off. Add the article to your course reading lists. Print off copies and make them available on your departmental noticeboard or outside your office for students or colleagues to browse and take away. You can have also have copies or the link available when you give departmental seminars or attend conferences.

There are many new technologies you can use to get your message out there—institutional or personal websites, Facebook, Twitter, Instagram and many others I probably don't know about.

If you are setting up your own website, make use of good advice from colleagues or experts. It needs to be targeted, focused, uncluttered, attractive and engaging. Be clear who your audience is and speak to them in ways that connect with their interests. Avoid too much text. It is better to use brief but catchy headlines and an enticing hook or summary with a link to read further if interested. Keep your website fresh but have a place to archive popular posts. You can use Google analytics or other programmes to give you data such as

> "By the time I had finished my PhD, I had attended several international conferences, published in two A grade international journals, was interviewed by journalists and had two news items published about my findings. Even at such a mature age, where many had retired, I felt a drive to 'just keep going' as I was committed to social justice for others. Maturity and experience provided the pillars and then being able to confidently share my views, without judgment, was so very important to me. But complacency is a word I don't use; more can be done." (JS, recent doctoral graduate)

number of individual visits, length of time spent on a page or clicks to following pages. I have a colleague who designs quirky quizzes based on his field of research. It makes people stay longer, frequently return to his site and forward links to their networks.

If you are going to upload YouTube clips, it doesn't take much to make these a little more professional. Try to get something between the stiff professor-sitting-at-a-desk look and the amateur-selfie-on-a-smartphone. Consider the look, sound and content quality. Getting the right lighting, angle and placement of your head and shoulders makes it easier to watch and absorb the content. Avoid recording in a place where noisy students pass by or jets fly overhead. Speak clearly and not too quickly without it sounding forced. Adopt a conversational tone and modulate your voice. Finally, have something worthwhile to say. Your clip should not be too long. The point you are making should be clear and the structure should be logical. If you are using a whiteboard, PowerPoint or other visual aid, try to integrate these seamlessly. Your video might require some editing but there are programmes you can download to help you with this. Ask your IT support team for assistance or useful tips.

Picking up on topical issues or commenting on another writer's blog are ways to keep up momentum when you are running out of topics to write about. A word of caution—if these blogs are linked to your work as an academic and you have career longevity in mind, pause, consider and check before you post.

"In terms of social media, my big piece of advice is to use what you think will be useful and what works for you. Personally, my preferences are Twitter and blogging; I have a personal Facebook [account] but if I'm honest, it's certainly never been a particularly professional venue for me. That doesn't mean they should be the same for everyone—pick what suits you and your research, and find the community of people working in your field. I've found Twitter particularly helpful for building a community of classicists at roughly the same career stage as me, and also for reaching out to people in other disciplines whose work I would not necessarily have known about by 'traditional' means—it's a great way of building interdisciplinarity." (LG, early career academic)

"If you want to tweet or blog under your research name, be serious. Let your research interests influence your blogging. Become a professional resource for people in your subfield. Be constructive and thoughtful not critical, and never use social media to attack colleagues. This will be a public good that pays back privately." (CB, early career academic)[19]

How do you influence policy and practice?

One of the reasons academics conduct research is to add new knowledge to the field. We can't all make amazing medical breakthroughs but there are other ways we can make a difference. Consider your doctoral thesis. It probably concluded with recommendations. How can you get some traction with these recommendations?

- Create an executive summary of your research that can be forwarded to policy makers or politicians.
- Create a blog post or YouTube clip and link to your executive summary.
- Write a short piece for your professional association's website or magazine.
- Write an opinion piece for your local newspaper.
- Contact your institution's communications officer to see if your findings might be of interest to your faculty or institution's website or their publicity material.
- Ask your institution's media contact if your findings might have a newsworthy angle.
- Make an appointment to meet with an influential policy maker, CEO, philanthropist or politician to explain the importance of your findings.
- Contact your alumni association as they often have publications that share what their members have done.
- Offer to speak at the next meeting of your subject association or professional group.

Having made that long list of ways to get your research out there, I do need to note that just because you are passionate about what you do, doesn't mean that other people will necessarily be. To engage their interest:

- Tailor it to your audience.
- Make key points without distracting detail.
- Have an 'angle' that will capture the interest of your audience.
- Link to current policy, practice or other issues in the field.
- Don't be defensive (or disappointed) if you don't get the reaction or level of interest you had hoped for.

How do you engage with the media?

My colleagues in communications tell me that very few academic stories get picked up by mainstream media. Getting media exposure usually happens in one of two ways: (a) you have a story that has broad appeal and is noticed by an online news service or a news franchise that has local or national newspapers, radio and television channels; or (b) you are approached by the media to comment on an item within your area of expertise.

My colleagues also tell me that many academics are cautious of the media or lack the confidence to be interviewed. My dealings with the media, across radio, television and print, have always been positive. The idea that they will grill you aggressively or deliberately quote you out of context has not been borne out in my experience. I have found newspaper and magazine reporters and radio and television hosts genuinely interested in what I have to say. They have asked a wide range of questions to understand the context and relevance of my topic. You will be interviewed because you are an expert on your topic and there is no reason for a reporter to try to 'catch you out'. They want an item that makes an interesting contribution to their programme or feature and are more likely to want to put you at ease.

Having said that, an hour interview might come to nothing. You might have all your words of wisdom reduced to two lines. The reporter needs to have an angle to their story that holds all the various contributions together. They might focus on things that you thought were not important or pick a sound bite that makes you sound less than articulate. They might use an old stock photograph of you that makes you cringe. I work from the idea that I am helping them do their job (provide an interesting story for their readers or listeners) and that my research might get some coverage at the same time. If it doesn't go as I had hoped, then I remind myself that 'today's newspaper is tomorrow's fish and chip wrapper' and that I am the only person who will probably remember.

There are some things that you can do to be sure you are well prepared. If a reporter contacts you and asks for an interview or comment, ask what particular angle they are interested in and say you will call back in 5 minutes. This gives you time to prepare your response. You won't have time to rehearse but you can sort out your key message and some supporting examples or evidence. When the interview takes place, this helps keep you on track and assists you to gently return the interviewer to the points that you want to make. In general, they want a 'sound bite' that is a clear summary of your key point—so if you help them out it is a win-win situation. You are both professionals with a job to do and mutual support and respect goes a long way.

How do you exercise your critic and conscience role?

The role of New Zealand universities as the critic and conscience of society is enshrined in the Education Act 1989 (section 162(4)(a)(v)). This is quite a responsibility and not one that sits comfortably with all academics. Some academics want to get on with their work and keep their heads down while others relish the opportunity to hold a mirror up to society in order to contribute to a more just world.

If you wish to use the opportunity to exercise your critic and conscience role, then many of the ideas already shared in this chapter could be used to approach this task. You can write a blog, a letter to the editor, an opinion piece for the newspaper, make a formal submission to a parliamentary select committee or exercise other forms of democratic expression. When you step outside the role of an academic content expert to become a political or societal commentator you can ruffle feathers so it is not a role you take on lightly. It helps if you do keep to areas in which you have expertise where your opinion has a basis in your research or experience. It is important not to use this opportunity to grandstand personal opinions or make personal attacks on those with differing opinions. Used judiciously and thoughtfully, this is one of the privileges of an academic role and should be valued.

Chapter 16 Developing your leadership

Te amorangi ki mua, te hapai o ki muri

The leader at the front and the workers behind the scenes

- What is meant by leadership capabilities?
- How do you develop leadership in teaching?
- How do you develop leadership in research?
- How do you develop leadership in and through service?
- What is the place of collaborative leadership?

What is meant by leadership capabilities?

"Leadership can be developed in many ways, e.g., supporting capacity development amongst your peers." (JW, senior academic)

The whakataukī at the top of the page reminds us that while there is often only one visible leader or spokesperson, leaders do not do it all by themselves, they are supported by a team of people working away in the background.

Viewed this way, everyone contributes to the leadership of their organisation. Everyone has a part to play, everyone's input is valued and everyone has strengths that can be recognised and enhanced.

There is a vast body of literature on all kinds of leadership approaches. Different styles seem to come and go, in and out of fashion—distributive leadership, authentic leadership, servant leadership, cultural leadership and e-leadership—the list goes on. A survey I read recently, however, claimed that four behaviours account for almost 90% of leadership effectiveness:

Solving problems effectively	The process that precedes decision-making is problem solving, when information is gathered, analysed and considered.
Supporting others	Leaders who are supportive understand and sense how other people feel. By showing authenticity and a sincere interest in those around them, they build trust and inspire and help colleagues to overcome challenges.
Seeking different perspectives	This trait is conspicuous in managers who monitor trends affecting organisations, grasp changes in the environment, encourage employees to contribute ideas that could improve performance, accurately differentiate between important and unimportant issues, and give the appropriate weight to stakeholder concerns.
Operating with a results orientation	Leadership is about not only developing and communicating a vision and setting objectives but also following through to achieve results. Source: Adapted from: http://www.mckinsey.com/global-themes/leadership/decoding-leadership-what-really-matters

My institution has recently introduced a leadership framework. It is now expected that these leadership dimensions are addressed in promotion applications. I have outlined the dimensions in the following table so that if your institution has not articulated its leadership expectations you can use these instead as a guide.

Dimension	Description	Examples
Exhibiting Personal Leadership Rangatiratanga	Role modelling leadership behaviours to engage others and support the University's values and aspirations.	Displaying personal qualities of courage, willingness to help others, collegiality, active listening; interpersonal relationships; active support for your leader or manager
Setting Direction Mana Tohu	Establishing and committing to plans and activities that will deliver the University's strategy.	Engagement in strategic planning or stakeholder engagement; evaluating feedback and making adjustments
Innovating and Engaging Whakamatāra	Identifying, creating and responding to relationships and opportunities to improve and progress the University.	Trying new teaching approaches; engaging in entrepreneurial activities; building relationships with community
Enabling People Hāpai	Developing self, others and teams so they can realise the University's strategy and values.	Leading a team; chairing meetings; advocating for equity; mentoring or coaching others
Achieving Results Whai hua Source: https://www.staff.auckland.ac.nz/en/human-resources/career-development/leadership-framework.html	Accepting accountability for making decisions and taking action to deliver the University's strategy and deliver excellent results.	Problem solving; decision making; responsibility for putting plans into action; reporting on achievement of goals

How do you develop leadership in teaching?

It is possible to display leadership at any level of teaching. As a tutor or graduate teaching assistant you can share good ideas and activities with other tutors, mentor new tutors, model good teaching and assessment practices and generally act in a collegial manner. Once you have more responsibility for a course you can display leadership in course development or review. You can model how to evaluate student feedback and make adjustments to the course. You can introduce new and innovative practices. As a course co-ordinator you can mentor tutors, markers and new lecturers. When you have more confidence, you can join your departmental or faculty teaching and learning committee. You can model willingness to improve your practice by working with your institution's centre for teaching and learning. As your skills and willingness are noticed by others, you may be asked to act as an external moderator for a course, be part of a qualification monitoring panel or contribute to a teaching showcase. If teaching is something that really excites you, you can enrol in further qualifications in tertiary teaching, undertake research into your own or others' teaching, attend conferences on the Study of Teaching and Learning (SoTL) and write for higher education journals.

"I go into the field. I'm a field biologist after all. I got into plant ecology because I like nature and being in the field observing patterns and processes. So, I make time (frequently) to go into the field to continue to hone my craft. I find observing plants, away from the distraction of the office admin, is where I have my best ideas. It's where I can mentor students, engage with managers, and see how the research we do in the Lab impacts. I get excited by ideas in the field and probably wouldn't be in academia if my main source of inspiration was removed." (JM, mid-career academic)

Similarly, you can develop leadership in your research and clinical or practicum supervision. While you will probably begin by being mentored and coached by others, you can return the favour by always being aware of those coming along behind you. You can pass on tips and material that might make their start easier. You can work up to becoming a mentor and lead supervisor yourself—always remembering what it was like when you started out. You can display leadership by offering support to students, such as inviting them to co-present or co-publish, or join groups or networks outside of the formal supervision sessions.

I bring all the students I supervise together as a cohort so they can meet each other, talk about common matters, such as applying for ethical approval or preparing for examination. Part of introducing them to each other is the expectation that those who are more experienced can pass their wisdom on to those who are just starting out.

How do you develop leadership in research?

If you have completed your PhD, you have already amassed a wide range of knowledge and skill related to the research process. You will have given seminars, attended conferences and written papers. If you are part of a research team or centre you will also have experienced applying for grants. All these experiences place you in a good position to begin to develop your research leadership. Don't just think about the content of your research, think also about all the theoretical, methodological, ethical and practical problems you encountered and solved along the way. One of my doctoral students faced particularly tricky ethical issues while undertaking her doctoral research. She used this experience to take her in unexpected directions as she wrote several articles, post-doctorate, on the ethics of doing research in her context. She shared her experience in our Emerging Scholars Forums and more widely to get others to rethink the nature of ethical decision making throughout a study.

Once you have gained experience in different aspects of planning, conducting and disseminating research, think about how you can share what you have gained with others through seminars, mentoring, giving advice or assistance or acting as a critical friend to others. You could set up your own reading or writing group.

Another way to build your leadership in research and to enable you to take advantage of different opportunities or initiatives that come your way is to attend the various professional development sessions. Institutions often run seminars or panels on grant writing, especially

> "Another aspect of her mentorship that has been of great benefit has been her regular 'research group' meetings. [Our supervisor] regularly gathers her PhD and Masters students to discuss aspects of the research process. This has provided me with an opportunity to learn from the expertise of others and to discuss aspects of the research journey in a safe and supportive small group environment."
> (DC, doctoral candidate)

> "Have one or two critical friends whose writing and work you respect highly to assist you in your research journey and to read your work."
> (GM, early career academic)

for the big funds, such as Marsden, Ako Aotearoa or, in my discipline, the Teaching and Learning Research Initiative. Apply for departmental, faculty or university grants to become familiar with the process. You might even be successful, as most institutions have funds set aside for new and emerging academics (see Chapter 8).

In order to be successful with larger grants, you will probably need to work as part of a team. The team might consist of colleagues in your department or you might extend it to include others from other faculties in your field (cross-faculty) or from other complementary fields (cross-discipline). If you are not the principal investigator (PI), you can still show leadership by taking the lead in a particular aspect of the process—organising a team meeting, managing the documentation or completing the relevant ethics approval. This builds your skills, takes pressure of the PI (who is probably a busy person anyway) and your willingness to step up might get you noticed by others.

How do you develop leadership in *and* through *service?*

Chapter 11 provides plenty of examples of how you can meet your service expectations. You can also use these opportunities to develop your personal leadership. As you complete these activities, you will be able to see leadership opportunities arising. You might begin by offering to stand in for someone while they are absent before taking on a longer-term role. Learning to chair committees, write position papers or review programmes are all activities that contribute to developing leadership skills. Your institution might have leadership programmes available—these are not always for academics wanting to be Deans or other senior leaders. There might be training opportunities for emerging leaders, Māori or Pacific leaders or women in leadership. When you are completing your appraisal or performance development interviews, ask your manager or mentor what leadership opportunities might be suitable for you. As a Head of School, I was always looking for academics to represent our school on faculty committees or degree development working parties. If you let people know of your interest, they can keep you in mind when vacancies arise.

Opportunities might exist outside your institution, through your professional body or discipline association, on conference committees or editorial boards. Your links into industry or the community might also provide leadership openings.

What is the place of collaborative leadership?

Not everyone sees leadership as an individual pursuit. For cultural, disciplinary, social or personal reasons, some people prefer to see leadership as a collaborative activity. In this neoliberal climate where individualism is prized, we need to work harder to recognise the personal and institutional benefits of collaborative ways of doing things and in recognising those behind the scenes who enable someone else to shine.

Whether it is a choice to lead in a distributed manner or whether it is just 'the way things are done', it helps to recognise what collaborative leadership looks like and how it contributes to achieving institutional goals. The focus is on relationships as much as on the achievement of the goal (in leadership jargon that means 'relational' as well as 'transactional'). Here are some characteristics:

- Collaborative leadership is based on a set of shared, often cultural, values.
- The agreed vision of the group is paramount.
- Tasks and roles are shared around in ways that recognise skill, status or fairness.
- People work together to achieve the goal regardless of who is the nominated leader.
- Group members focus on the efforts of others rather than drawing attention to themselves.
- People often sacrifice their own recognition or achievement for the sake of others or the group.

> "As a Samoan, I envisage Pasifika leadership in higher education to be committed to the spirit of the collective. This means that Pasifika leaders are concerned with growing leadership capacity in others. This means you do not always put your individual interests first. Pasifika leadership is about humility and understanding (of self and others) 'Tofa sa'ili'—a balance of harmony in search for wisdom and knowledge." (JaM, early career academic)

> "Interactions in the two Māori organisations indicated an awareness of the importance of humility and a tendency to emphasise the group over the individual. Māori leaders tended to tell stories about how they learned from their mistakes, rather than the kind of 'hero' stories often heard in Pākehā workplaces. And when something needed to be improved, or someone had made an error, the Māori leaders were more likely to talk about the issue as a general one, even discussing it with humour where possible, rather than pointing the finger at an individual." (Research on Māori leadership)[20]

- Each group member's effort is recognised and valued within the group.
- Problems are shared and solved by the group.

A leadership blog I read recently had some provocative suggestions that fit with some of the points being made in this section. I have taken some of the headings and provided some ideas for the academic context:

Leading up the chain	In what ways do you support your leaders and managers? How do you model support for those who have to make decisions? You don't need to be insincere but you can avoid undermining someone who is doing their best.
Taking extreme ownership	This means always asking yourself what part you played in something that did not succeed rather than looking for someone else to blame. It means that you make sure that you are clear about expectations before taking on a task.
Being proactive and not reactive	Not rushing into things but stopping to consider the possible consequences and how you might mitigate these will lead to improved chances of success. When it doesn't go well see it as another opportunity to get it right.
Passing the credit to others	A good leader gives credit to others when things go well and shoulders responsibility when things don't go so well. It is also important to acknowledge that things work well when everyone plays their part no matter how small.
Stepping back to make opportunities for others	A good leader knows when their time has passed and it is time to pass the baton. This handover process is done in a way that sets the new leader up for success. Source: Adapted from https://www.linkedin.com/pulse/what-leadership-parag-kar

Chapter 17 Managing the demands

He moana pukepuke, e ekengia e te waka

A choppy sea can be navigated

- What can you expect in your first few years?
- How do you fit it all in?
- How do you maintain a life outside?
- Where do you go for help?

What can you expect in your first few years?

You are excited to hook that first job in academia. You want to make a good impression, especially if it is only a short-term contract. You are still finding your way around, learning people's names and roles, all the while trying to live out of a suitcase until you find a new flat. You are given your teaching timetable and while it might only be a couple of courses, every class is brand new for you and they take hours of preparation.

My best advice is to be gentle with yourself. Yes, you will feel overwhelmed but you will also feel exhilarated. Try to hold on to the good times to get you through the down times. I remember the exhaustion of my first

> *"Becoming an academic means you're doing research (and guiding student projects) and teaching (which includes marking, subject co-ordination, subject review, student interactions, etc.). You're also expected to write grants, serve on a myriad of committees, advise students and review the work of others (manuscripts, proposals). Each of these can take up a lot of your time each day. And there is only so much time in the day to get everything done." (JM, mid-career academic)*

academic position. I only had 12 hours face-to-face teaching a week but everything was so new. I had to find my way around the campus, get used to unfamiliar technology and teach courses I had never taught before with no notes from the previous lecturer to guide me. I even had to teach a course outside my area of expertise, which required me to do endless reading to get up to speed. I was then expected to arrive in class as if I had it all under control and knew everything about the subject matter.

You would have thought I might have learned from that early experience but when I arrived in my current position, it was much the same. I taught a course I had never taught before and because I didn't understand how the programme worked, I followed the course outline and assessment schedule—but no one told me that the assignments were previously marked by a team of three. I ended up with 2 x 200 assignments to mark over 2 weeks while conducting individual interviews with every student in the class. I wondered what had hit me.

> "**What I wish someone had told me:** I wish that someone had said: Don't panic! In the middle of my first full semester of teaching I panicked, the teaching workload seemed impossible and I was falling further and further behind with my research and writing. By the second semester, I had a sense of when the most intensely busy periods were likely to be, and accepted that some jobs would need to wait for less-busy times. Perhaps, however, even if someone had told me this, I wouldn't have fully understood the rhythm of the academic year until I had experienced it."
> (MM, early career academic)

The difference this time was that I had the confidence to speak up, ask for help and check the expectations for the next courses that were assigned to me so that I could manage the workload more reasonably. You will, as the early career academic above notes, get to understand the flow of the academic year. You can try negotiating with your academic head to allocate teaching in ways that give you space to do other things. This might be trying to ensure you have at least one day a week clear of teaching and service duties. Or you might like to teach summer school to free up a block of time later in the year. Talk to experienced colleagues to see how they manage their time.

Another thing that often happens when you are new is that you are assigned the courses that no-one else wants to teach—those large compulsory undergraduate courses that seem to generate lots of student dissatisfaction, often beyond your control. You can deal with this in several ways: grin and bear it knowing that you can pass it on to the next new lecturer; speak up and ask for support, especially given that you are new to the role; or use it as a learning opportunity—listen to the student concerns and make changes to the course to make it more engaging and relevant. The last option is the most satisfying but most exhausting one.

Many of the academics, both new and experienced, who have provided advice for this book, have emphasised how teaching will expand to fit all the time you have available if you let it. You need to know when to stop your preparation, how to refine your marking and ways to manage student queries so these tasks do not eat into time allocated to other activities.

In the first few years you will run the gamut of emotions. You will be thrilled to be starting your new position. You will be proud of the achievements that got you to this point. You will be excited to be meeting new colleagues, especially ones whose work you have admired. You will get a buzz from your teaching and you will probably drive your partner/family/flatmates to distraction talking about your new job.

> "You can't do everything. Work out priorities and keep a note of the time you allocate to them. Teaching can take up a lot of time—but having a couple of hours each day to write is also important. " (JW, senior academic)

You will also be anxious about doing things properly, nervous each time you meet a new group of students, exhausted from your never-ending workload and worried that you don't seem to be making headway with your research and writing schedule.

> "Near the 6-month mark I realized that different opportunities will come up for different people at different times. My turn will come too." (JT, early career academic)

It does settle down but there are strategies you can use to get through. It helps to find a colleague or group of colleagues inside your institution or friend outside that you trust and can debrief with. This is one of the purposes of the Emerging Scholars Forum—the members know what it's like and can be useful sounding boards and even suggest practical solutions. Other strategies in this book might also alleviate some of the anxiety or help you streamline planning and manage expectations.

All the advice about getting enough sleep, eating healthily, finding time for exercise and time to switch off from work are even more important. Get into good habits and routines now and they will support you through your first year and set the groundwork for other stressful times that you might face as your career moves forward. You need to manage the job not let the job manage you.

How do you fit it all in?

We have already talked about learning when to say 'no' (in Chapters 3 and 4). Often in your eagerness to please you take on extra work or agree to tasks that you don't really have time for.

Don't try to solve problems that are not yours. Refer the person to the staff member with the responsibility or expertise. Don't make promises you can't keep—provide a realistic timeframe by which you can complete the task or politely decline.

> "If you are unable to take on extra work, say so—don't be afraid to say no. It's far more desirable to successfully complete your existing work load than to take on extra work, deal with that unsatisfactorily and stress yourself out in the process." (UTS website)

The research tells us that multi-tasking is not an effective strategy. Start your new position by ditching some of those old habits and setting up new routines. I find my biggest time wasters are emails. If you are like my son, you spent your student years working on your assignments with Facebook, Gmail, YouTube and a computer game all open at once and you switched between them all. Take time now to make your computer time distraction-free. Here are my suggestions:

- Turn off the functions (beeps, pings and pop-up windows) that tell you a new email has arrived—and you can similarly turn off annoying functions on your phone (but you might like to keep meeting reminders).
- Don't subscribe to apps on your work email address that constantly send updates and offers.
- To avoid email clutter, don't connect Facebook, LinkedIn, ResearchGate or similar sites to your work email.
- Set times in your day (and put them in your diary) when you will attend to emails (for example, first thing in the morning or after lunch).
- Use the sorting functions on Outlook or your email system—these enable you to sort into folders, prioritise or colour-code incoming emails.

- Avoid multiple handling. I suggest that you learn to filter quickly: delete, file or respond.
- If you accidentally delete an important email, don't panic—you can check your deleted file or wait until someone sends you a reminder.
- You don't need to respond to emails when you are only copied in for information.
- You might like to add a footnote to your email signature that says you will endeavour to respond within a certain time frame (for example, 48 hours)—this lessens the expectation of an instant reply.
- Avoid the all-staff email list function—constant emails about irrelevant things can be really irritating. If you have a staff intranet or newsletter make better use of those.
- Use your out-of-office function to tell people when you are absent and who to contact instead.

Another possible time waster is dealing with student queries—via email, through your student communication system or at your office door. An open door policy or anytime email habit might seem student-friendly but it is not a good use of your time and doesn't train your students to try to solve their own problems.

When I am introducing myself to students, I also tell them about reasonable communication expectations. I let them know which email address or system works best. I tell them that I will endeavour to get back to them within 3 days but if they haven't heard within that timeframe to re-send the email as it might have slipped down my in-box. I tell them my office hours or how to set up an appointment. I suggest that if it is a minor query, they try other avenues first, such as other students in the class, the course webpage, the library or the student centre. If they need to talk to me about a more serious, personal or detailed matter, they are best to make an appointment where I can give them my full attention rather than try to catch me after class, as I might need to head off to a meeting or another class.

> "Keep work boundaries—make sure you are not available all the time. Emailing students at 9pm basically tells them that you are always available. Even if you have to write your emails at night on occasion, write these as drafts and send first thing in the morning. This at least gives the impression to others of your hours that you are at work."
> (JM, early career academic)

Another time waster can be colleagues who want to drop by and chat and don't know when to leave. You don't want be seen as rude or standoffish and these might be the very people you need to seek help from one day. In my school we have an unwritten rule that if a colleague's door is shut that they are either not there, are in a meeting or occupied with a task that requires their full concentration. You can knock and if they are available for a brief query they will come to the door to assist you. If they have more time they might invite you in. If it is a brief hello or query, then you are expected to leave after a few minutes. This might sound draconian but it had become so bad that some staff members were locking their doors and turning out their lights out so a colleague wouldn't constantly interrupt them. Setting these ground rules helped change the culture without increasing stress. We all felt better about preserving our important office time.

Other strategies are to put a notice on your door to say something like: "If my door is shut, please respect that I am fully occupied by another task. If it's important send me an email." In another school in my faculty, they have clock faces on their doors where the hands point to options such as "At a meeting", "Teaching a class", "Off-campus", "Busy", "Available, please knock." I don't feel as comfortable with this strategy because I don't think anyone needs to account to their colleagues for their whereabouts but it might work for you. If you want to have chats with people, you could take the initiative to invite them for a coffee at a time that suits you both. I always like it when people ask me to do this.

> "Not only will academic publishing not make you famous, rich or more interesting, but anyone attempting to write will have to juggle that with an increasingly demanding workload. Amongst the ever-increasing teaching, tutoring, marking and administration tasks that are demanded of you, where will you find time to write?" (CD & NL, senior academics)

Once you have eliminated distractions you can then plan to maximise the time you have at your disposal. I like the week-at-a-glance view in my diary. First I put in things I cannot change like lectures or meetings I'm expected to attend. I include time before and after these events for travel, preparation or reading minutes, agendas and papers. I put in matters that have made it to the priority pile—things with set deadlines or that impact on someone else's ability to complete their next step. I then look for blocks of time I can take for research, reading or writing. If I have assignments to mark I also find blocks of time for this task. I make some times available for student supervisions and meetings. I try to fit everything else in and around those key times.

You will get better at judging how long tasks take and you will find what works for you—what time of day is best for certain things and how to block in certain tasks to free up other slots. I hate to say it but you will find your work encroaching into non-work time. Negotiate this with your family and try to stick to the agreements you make. One trick I used was sitting down with my school-aged son and we both did our "homework" together. It set good habits in place for him and I got things done but I could still be with him to answer his queries.

> *"The biggest problem I faced: When do you read? In my first year I have found it incredibly hard to find time for substantial reading. This was partly because I was a new mum and my time was not as flexible as it had been. I read student work and the required texts for the courses I was teaching on, but struggled to find time to sit and read the latest journal articles, and the pile of books 'to read' on my desk got taller and taller. I would love to know when other academics get their reading done, particularly those with family responsibilities out of work."* (MM, early career academic)

How do you maintain a life outside academia?

At first, you will think that it is not possible to have a life outside academia but with good planning, time management and a bit of self-discipline you can do it. As I have noted earlier, the first 6 to 12 months will be exhausting and overwhelming. This is an important time to set those routines in place—at work and at home.

> *"Enjoy your work. Build relationships. Keep up interests outside of work. Spend time with those who matter to you."* [KF, senior academic]

Without wanting to sound like a life coach or relationship counsellor, you need to put as much effort into other aspects of your life as you do your work. I don't mean that you need to timetable every minute of your non-work time but you do need to make space for the important activities and relationships that will sustain you.

First, there is taking care of yourself. Yes, you might need to burn the midnight oil occasionally to get that funding application completed or thesis marked but these should be the exception. More and more research is emphasising the importance of regular patterns of sufficient sleep. The research will also tell you about healthy eating—what, when and how to eat. And, of course, you can treat yourself—I find it really helps to get through that pile of undergraduate essays if I mark ten then reward myself with something tasty.

The other important health-related activity is exercise. For some it's cycling to work; for others a session at the gym. I'm not a gym person so I try to build exercise into my regular routines—walking during the week and swimming on the weekends. If you take part in a sport, try to keep it up. There will be social as well as physical benefits to disconnecting from work and engaging fully in something you enjoy. You might not think you have time for much else but it is important to find ways that help you switch off—listening to or playing music, spending time with your family, cooking exotic dishes, practising your religion, working in the garden or keeping up a community activity. It doesn't have to be a huge time commitment—I find that I can lose myself very quickly in Sudoku and cup of Earl Grey tea.

Second, is taking care of your relationships—partners, family and extended family, friends and community. There is an old adage that says, "No-one on their deathbed ever wished they'd spent more time at work." Again, research tells us that sustaining relationships requires time and effort. We shouldn't take our partners, parents, children or other significant support people for granted. Sure, we have stressful and demanding jobs but we are well paid, have good conditions of work and a lot of autonomy over our time.

Our institutions have HR policies around parental leave and flexible working hours. Many have childcare centres attached. You can negotiate timeframes and workloads (within reason) with your academic head so that you can work from home at certain times or leave early to collect your children from school. You can apply for periods of research and study leave or special leave. It is up to you to use this time, and

> "Make time for family and friends. At the end of the day, they get us through the lows in life, and share our highs. Don't neglect them because you have 'urgent' work to do. That should be done in work time. I've found that working 70 hrs a week isn't actually very productive. I reckon I work 50 hrs a week and even this is probably too much. Weekends are 'me time' as best I can manage. I haven't always done this but I'm seeing the benefit of getting away from academia and enjoying life. For me, that's wooden boats (I have a plan to build one soon), sailing and bushwalking. Surprisingly, I usually come to work on Mondays all invigorated and happy, and that can only be a good thing for my health, sanity and productivity. (JM, mid-career academic)

your non-work time, in a relationship/family friendly way. I spend my weekdays in one city (my workplace) and my weekends and holidays in another (my home). One thing I have learnt over the years is that in a relationship you need be interested in the small things as well as the big things. My husband and I try to talk by Skype or Facetime every evening for half an hour. No matter what deadlines we each might have we prioritise this time so as to not lose touch with those small but important everyday things. I don't see that it is any different when you are living in the same house. Do your important people get some focused uninterrupted time to spend time with you?

Where do you go for help?

There will be times when you feel you are sinking under the strain. Step back and see if you are doing too much. Are you doing things that could be delegated or could be forwarded to someone else? Do you need to adjust your planning, expectations or deadlines? Are you making the best use of services that are available to you? Have you read the relevant policies? Do you need to ask for help?

Start with colleagues or mentors. It might be that you just need to debrief and that in the articulation of the problem you work out your own solution. When you find out that others are frustrated by the same issue or have met that issue before, you can discuss possible ways forward together. You might also find that there are other people or systems to help you.

> "*Use your resources.* This includes making sure you're getting most from your university's benefits for employees; talking to the library to make sure you know all they can do for you and your students; asking colleagues if you can watch them lecture to get ideas and a sense of the 'house style'; reading any minutes of meetings that come your way to get a sense of how things work without actually being involved; going to staff development workshops or training events for new tech[nology]." (LG, early career academic)

Does your institutional intranet have an FAQ or A-Z page? Is there a central helpline? Can your administrator, HR or IT person help you?

If you need to talk to a programme leader, academic head or other senior staff member, make an appointment and take the issue, its consequences and some possible solutions with you. It might be that you can be offered tutorial or marking support or that someone else can teach that course. Most people in these positions want to help you find a solution. It might be a problem that needs to go to a staff meeting or the relevant committee but at least there will be more heads than just yours searching for a way forward.

If it is a problem meeting a research or writing deadline, contact the research leader or editor. You will probably find that you are not the only one struggling and the deadline can be pushed out or support offered to relieve your stress.

If it is a student-related matter, there will be a Student Dean or Programme Leader that you can talk to. It might be a problem that can be solved easily or it might be more serious. If a possible outcome is that a student could be reprimanded or dismissed, you must make yourself familiar with the relevant policies and follow these to the letter. There is usually a policy or flow chart outlining what should happen and in what order. Don't try to do it by yourself. Involve the staff member with the responsibility for these matters earlier rather than later.

Similarly, if you have a problem with another staff member, whose behaviour includes sexual harassment, racist remarks or workplace bullying, don't try to ignore it or manage it by yourself. There are people who can help you, such as HR, your academic head or your counselling service. Make yourself familiar with the grievance policy and procedures. Stay calm and keep notes or collect evidence of the problem that you can pass on to the person who will help you with the process. By dealing with the problem, you will make it better for others as well as yourself.

If you have a personal matter or an issue at home impacting on your ability to do your job properly, you can go to your academic head or to HR. Most institutions are signed up to a staff support programme such as EAP (Employee Assistance Programme), where you or your family member can receive relevant counselling or advice (and the first session is paid for by the institution). If you find that despite seeking advice or receiving help that you can't pull yourself out the dark hole you are in, then you must seek professional help. Start with your family doctor in case it is a medical problem that can be dealt with easily. If your doctor feels you need psychological or specialist care they can refer you on. Your institution might have a health and counselling service that you can use. These services are always confidential and no one needs to know what you are trying to cope with unless you choose to tell them.

While your down times will be rare, you need to know that you are not the only one who has felt like this. If you have taken the advice in this book, you will have built up networks of support and have good strategies in place to manage the peaks and troughs. If, finally, you feel that academia is not for you, you take a range of useful skills and experiences that will stand you in good stead in many other occupations. If you are able to see your way through the bumpy patches, you will come to find that academia offers many rich and rewarding experiences and a sense of a having made a worthwhile contribution to society both now and in the future.

Chapter 18 Setting up your own Emerging Scholars Forum

He waka eke noa

A canoe that we are all in together

- How do you find out what support is already available?
- How do you determine if there is interest in forming your own group?
- How do set up your own Emerging Scholars Forum?

How do you find out what is already available?

Many new and emerging scholars are already provided with induction programmes—both at institutional and departmental levels. My experience is that induction programmes focus more on operational matters and expectations. More recently, institutions have begun to provide mentors and mentoring programmes to assist new academics. These vary in length and depth but generally give new academics an introduction to expectations and goal setting across their teaching, research and service. Such programmes often complement appraisal or continuation processes. In some cases new academics are brought together to be introduced to support systems and network with each other. For new academics who are part of established research centres or programmes, their induction is often very hands-on.

Many informal groups also spring up. Across my faculty there are reading, writing and discussion groups. They might be initiated by experienced academics with an interest in a particular theorist (such as Deleuze), or methodology (such as narrative inquiry). They are a great way to meet colleagues from across the faculty and be introduced to a community of scholars with similar interests. Our school also has off-site intensive writing weeks both for staff and for doctoral students. Investigate what your institution has to offer and give it a try to see what works for you.

How do you determine if there is interest in forming your own group?

The idea of an Emerging Scholars Forum is not designed to replace any of these existing models. It has a different function. Rather than focusing on setting individual goals or meeting specific purposes, it aims to bring together emerging academics at a similar stage in their careers to discuss what matters to them. A stocktake of what is available might show that emerging scholars are well catered for and that there is no need for another group to be established; or it might identify a gap where new and emerging academics feel they are overwhelmed or isolated and need to talk to people who understand what they are going through.

It pays first to establish a need and a fit. Talk to other emerging academics in your department, and further afield if you have established networks. You could send out a brief survey or call a meeting to canvass interest. Get your library or bookstore to stock this book so that the idea gets around. Discuss the idea with your academic staff development centre who might find it a useful complement to their work. Drop the idea into conversations and discuss how such a forum might work in your faculty or institution. It might take some time from sowing the first seeds to seeing your idea come to fruition.

All good ideas need someone to champion them. Unless someone puts up their hand to manage communication, organise meetings, invite guests and facilitate

"The group provided a scaffold I needed to support my transition from doctoral student to an emerging scholar within a university. For, as a doctoral student I learnt the art of academic research, but not the fullness of what an academic career entails. Having senior academics leading the group, creating a collegial community between emerging scholars - and, at times, inviting 'expert' guests (such as the University's media advisor) to present, seemed to be the right mix. It's nice to know you are not alone, and that the things I need to know as an emerging scholar are not a mystery." (AS, early career academic) discussion, it will just remain a good idea. An emerging scholar might want to get the process underway to determine what the participants would find useful and how the group might operate. A more senior colleague, with an interest in mentoring, might take this role on by themselves or in conjunction with an emerging scholar.

How do you set up an Emerging Scholars Forum?

The Forum might operate in a more fluid and collaborative manner with individuals taking responsibility for different aspects or facilitating particular sessions. It will be important to engage more experienced colleagues at some stage because they have key institutional knowledge, significant experience, useful advice and established networks. Talking to your Head of Department or Dean might help you gain institutional support and financial resources to set up and sustain the Forum's momentum.

There will be a few key decisions to make once the need for such a forum is established. I have listed some important questions in the table below. Beside that I have noted how I got my first Emerging Scholars Forum off the ground. The fact that our original Emerging Scholars Forum is still continuing years after it started is testament to it being a useful concept. As members moved on, others appeared to fill their places. There are no hard and fast rules for what will work in another setting but at the most basic level, each of the chapters in this book can be conversation starters in forum meetings. Forum members can share their experiences, ask questions or give advice. They can engage their more senior colleagues in wider dialogue and debate. Other matters might arise given changes in government or institutional policy or as someone brings a matter to the group that they wish discussed. At our most recent meeting, the group decided to take political action about representation of new and emerging scholars in decision-making on a faculty-related matter—and took their concerns as far as the Vice-Chancellor. It wasn't something that I had anticipated would be a role for the group but when I reflect on their action, I am reminded of one the themes I introduced in the first chapter, that *academic life provides you with great privilege but also has great responsibility.* If I have contributed to my new and emerging scholars gaining confidence with their place in the institution and

Questions to consider	How it worked for us
1. Who will be invited to participate? Who constitutes the group you would consider new and emerging scholars—new appointments, recent doctoral graduates, doctoral candidates planning on an academic career?	• To get my first forum off the ground, I invited new academics that I had employed as Head of School and/or taught or supervised with, and colleagues who were not so new but were completing PhDs, along with doctoral candidates who I knew were considering academic careers. The concept of a new and emerging scholar was loose and fluid. It was an eclectic group and included emerging scholars from across the faculty. Participants came if and when it suited them and joined and left as they wished. One of our first participants didn't leave until he became an associate professor.
2. How will your participants be recruited? By open invitation, nomination from others, word-of-mouth or through more formal channels such as HR or mentoring programmes?	• Everyone in my first group was invited by me, personally. When a participant asked, "why was I invited?", I said, "because you had crossed my path and I thought you might get something from this group." Later, others asked to join, were invited by current participants or nominated by their Heads of School. Some were part of other groups, such as the formal university mentoring scheme, but they liked the fact that this one group was not a 'requirement' or tied to their continuation or appraisal.
3. How will the group be led—by an enthusiastic new academic, by a group of supportive colleagues or by a senior colleague?	• In order for such a group to succeed it needs at least one person who is committed to it and places high priority on making it succeed. In the case of our first group, that was me. It helped that I was a senior academic with a wide range of experiences and access to networks and resources. A colleague who was an emerging academic was also able to get an interested group of people together at another institution to get a group underway.
4. How, when, where and how often should the group meet?	• We meet three to four times per year from generally from 4.30pm to 6pm on a day that suits most people's teaching commitments. We have varied the day and time of day to meet the needs of those who have family responsibilities or tight travel timetables.
5. What kind of format will work best for your meetings?	• We have a pattern we follow. The first half is less formal. We begin with a round-the-table informal catch-up. Participants share anything they think that might be of interest since we last met. The next section focuses on questions that they might have, problems that have arisen or good ideas they'd like to share. We take a short break for shared refreshments. The second half usually focuses on a key topic that we have agreed upon ahead of time and could include an invited speaker.
6. How formal do you want the expectations to be?	• In my group there were no expectations beyond attending when you could and engaging in a positive and collaborative manner. Participants could volunteer to take a turn to provide snacks, host a meeting or help organise a topic or speaker.

being energised by the collegial support of their peers to speak up, then I am satisfied my input has been worthwhile. The forum has met a need in our institution and I'm sure this book will be equally useful in other tertiary settings. Our new and emerging scholars are the future of academia; we must nurture, respect and value them.

Poipoia te kākano; Kia puawai
Nurture the seed and it will blossom

Notes

1. Ian Symonds (2013). Why be an academic? *O & G Magazine, 15*(3), 34–35 (cited with permission).
2. What do academics do? http://www.academiccareer.manchester.ac.uk/about/do/
3. Wicked problems are complex societal issues requiring new ways of thinking—attributed to Horst Rittel, (1973). Dilemmas in a General Theory of Planning. *Policy Sciences, 1973*, 155–169.
4. Liz Gloyn: https://lizgloyn.wordpress.com/2011/09/02/survival-tips-for-new-academics-like-me/ (cited with permission).
5. University of Technology Sydney: http://www.iml.uts.edu.au/develop-career/survival.html
6. John Morgan, *Advice for new academics [or what I reckon I've got right, and wrong]*: http://morganvegdynamics.blogspot.co.nz/2015/01/advice-for-new-academics-or-what-i.html (cited with permission).
7. Performance-Based Research Fund is a way of determining research quality and funding New Zealand tertiary institutions accordingly. It is conducted by the Tertiary Education Commission every 6 years: http://www.tec.govt.nz/funding/funding-and-performance/funding/fund-finder/performance-based-research-fund/
8. Ako Aotearoa, the National Centre for Tertiary Teaching Excellence: https://akoaotearoa.ac.nz/
9. *Kia Eke Panuku*: http://kep.org.nz/assets/resources/site/brochure-CR-RP.pdf
10. Te Kete Ipurangi: http://seniorsecondary.tki.org.nz/The-arts/Pedagogy/Culturally-responsive-learning-environments/Tangata-whenuatanga
11. *Ka Hikitia 2013–2017*: https://education.govt.nz/assets/Documents/Ministry/Strategies-and-policies/Ka-Hikitia/KaHikitiaAcceleratingSuccessEnglish.pdf
12. Tuakāna programme: https://www.auckland.ac.nz/en/on-campus/student-support/personal-support/academic-learning-support/tuakana.html
13. John Marsden (1998). *Prayer for the Twenty-first Century*. Star Bright Books.
14. Angus MacFarlane. (2010). *Huakina mai: Doorways toward culturally responsive education.* https://akoaotearoa.ac.nz/download/ng/file/group-3300/huakina-mai-doorways-toward-culturally-responsive-education.pdf

15 Carl Davidson & Neil Lunt. (2000). *The art of getting published. A guide for academics*. Palmerston North: Dunmore Press.

16 Phil Silva in Carl Davidson & Neil Lunt. (2000). *The art of getting published. A guide for academics*. Palmerston North: Dunmore Press.

17 Beall's List: https://scholarlyoa.com/2016/01/05/bealls-list-of-predatory-publishers-2016/

18 *He Rautaki mo te Akoranga Kairangi*. The-Nature-of-Doctoral-Supervision: http://www.tlri.org.nz/sites/default/files/projects/1.-9250-The-Nature-of-Doctoral-Supervision.pdf

19 Chris Blattman, *Advice for new assistant professors*: http://chrisblattman.com/2014/04/15/advice-new-assistant-professors/

20 http://www.victoria.ac.nz/lals/centres-and-institutes/language-in-the-workplace/research/maori-leadership

References

Kenway, J. Gough, N. & Hughes, M. (1998). *Publishing in academic journals: A pocket guide.* Geelong, Vic: Deakin Centre for Education and Change, Deakin University.

Mutch, C. (2005/2013). *Doing Educational Research. A practitioner's guide to getting started.* Wellington: NZCER Press.

Index

40/40/20 role 3, 92

abstracts, writing 64
Academia.edu 114
academic citizenship 4
academics
   benefits to an academic career 5–6
   description 2–4
   expectations of an early career academic 1–2, 4–5, 127–30
   positioning, to be considered for academic job 8–9
   reasons for becoming an academic 5
   responsibility 2
   variety of tasks 1–2
   where to go for help 135–37
accountability 6, 20
ako 49
Ako Aotearoa, National Tertiary Teaching Centre 41, 58, 109, 110, 124
applying for an early career academic position 11–12
appointment process 12–13
appointments committee 8, 12
assignments, preparation of students 37–40, 45–46

balance between profession and life outside academia 2, 23, 133–35
Beall's List of predatory publishers 74
bibliometrics 113–15
blogging 116, 117, 119
buddy 16, 106

career path in academia 3
career plan 20–22

citations, as measures of academic uptake 113–15
city—suburb—street structure for essays and exam questions 45–46
coaching 28, 29
   characteristics 27
colleagues
   discussing your problems with 135
   help to deal with problem colleagues 136
   interruptions from 132
collegiality 4, 46, 93, 122
committee work 22, 91, 92, 93, 105
   meeting etiquette 93–94
community commitments 23, 96
community service 92, 96–97
competition 2, 6, 20
concept web 35
conferences
   attending and presenting 99–101
   how to give a professional presentation 102
   networking and follow up 99, 103
   publishing in conference proceedings 103–04
confirmation
   cultural approaches 109–10
   evidence portfolio 107–09
   preparation 107
continuation 22
   cultural approaches 109–10
   evidence portfolio 107–09
   preparation 107
contracts 15
   part-time 105–06
   short-term 10, 105–06, 127
counselling 136
critic and conscience role 119
cultural approaches to confirmation and continuation 109–10

145

culturally responsive teaching 48–51
curriculum vitae (CV, resumé) 10, 11, 12, 58, 71, 73, 95, 99, 106, 115

diaries 132–33
dissemination of research 113
   critic and conscience role 119
   how to spread ideas more widely 115–16
   influencing policy and practice 117
   media 118–19
   publishing outlets, advantages and disadvantages 73–74
   research uptake 113–15
doctoral study
   see also supervision
   as a basis for building a research platform 54–56
   creative options 82
   examinations and other assessments 81–82
   statement describing a thesis 55, 58
'dual professionals' 3

EAP (Employee Assistance Programme) 136
Education Act 1989 119
emails 130–31
Emerging Scholars Forum 8, 17, 123, 129
Emerging Scholars Forum, forming a new group
   determining need and fit 139–40
   finding out what is already available 138–39
   setting up 140–41
engagement of students in tutorials 34–35
entry requirements for new academic 7–8

evidence portfolio 107–09
examinations
   doctoral candidates 81
   preparation of students 37–40, 45–46
expectations
   of an early career academic 4–5
   quantifiable 22
Expression of Interest (EoI) 59

Facebook 115, 116, 130
family life and commitments 23, 133, 134–35, 136
flipped teaching 53
focus 19
formative assignments 39
friends, making time for 134
future academic career 17–18

gender equity policies 14
glass ceilings 14
goals 20–22, 25, 106
Google Scholar 114, 115
group work 34–35

health 133–34
help with difficulties and problems 135–37

induction programmes 15–16, 138
interview 10, 12–13

job advertisement for new academic 7–8

Ka Hikitia strategy 49

leadership 3, 5
   capabilities 120–21

collaborative 125–26
dimensions 121
Māori 125
Pasifika 125
in research 123–24
in teaching 122–23
in and through service 124–25
lecture theatres 43–44
library services 9, 45, 92, 131, 135
LinkedIn 130

mana motuhake 49
manaakitanga 49
Māori
    academics 14
    community roles 96
    key concepts 49
    leaders 125
    promotion applications 111
    support programmes 49–50
    teaching and learning
        relationships 48–50
marking 9, 37, 39–40, 128, 129, 133, 134
Marsden Fast Start grants 57
Marsden Fund 124
media, engaging with 118–19
medicine, academic career 5
meeting etiquette 93–94
meetings 21–22
mentoring 5, 26–27, 41, 58, 95, 106, 122, 138
    characteristics 27
    cultural mentoring 49
    different kinds of mentors 27–28, 29
    expectations of a mentor 30–31
    finding a mentor 29–30
    formal programmes 30
    promotion applications 110, 111
    in research 27, 29, 81, 122, 123
    in service 29
    talking to mentors about problems 135
    in teaching 27, 29, 122

neoliberal ideologies 2, 6, 20
networking 30, 92, 99, 103, 115

online publications 75
online teaching 52
open access publishing 74–75, 114
opportunities, deciding whether to accept 18–19, 23, 24, 130
ōritetanga 49

panel discussions 101
part-time positions 10, 105–06
Pasifika
    academics 14
    community roles 96
    leaders 125
    promotion applications 111
    teaching and learning relationships 50
Pasifika Education Plan 50
PBRF (Performance-Based Research Fund) 8, 21, 22, 74, 75, 78, 81, 114
performance appraisal 106
plagiarism 87, 90
    self-plagiarism 63
policy, influencing 117
political commenting 119
polytechnics 3, 32
portfolios
    evidence portfolio 107–09
    teaching award portfolio 110
    teaching portfolio 40–41, 109

position expectations for new
    academic 7–8
poster presentation 100
PowerPoint presentations 44, 48, 102,
    114, 116
predatory journals and publishers 74–
    75
presentations
    deciding whether to accept
        opportunities 18–19
    how to give a professional
        presentation 102
    types 100–01
prior career experience and activities 17
priority setting 25, 129
probation period 106
professional development 16, 105, 106
Professional Teaching Fellows 3
promotion, applying for 110–12, 114
publications 4, 9, 22, 61
    see also writing
    book proposal 72–73
    conference proceedings 103–04
    determining authorship 76
    dissemination outlets, advantages
        and disadvantages 73–74
    how to get published 69–71
    maximising earlier work 61–63
    measuring readership 113–14
    PhD by or with publication 82
    rejections 77–79
    turning a thesis into a book 71–73
    typical publishing process 76–77

qualifications 7
    recognition of work experience 3

reading 133
recruitment process 10–11

referees 12
research 3, 4, 9, 17, 18
    see also dissemination of research;
        publications; supervision
    brief statement on field of
        research 18
    coaching 29
    deadlines 136
    deciding whether to accept
        opportunities 18–19, 24
    earlier work as a platform for
        developing research 54–56
    goals 22
    keeping up momentum 60
    leadership 123–24
    mentoring 27, 29, 81, 122
    new or complementary areas of
        research 56–57
    sponsoring 29
    statement of prior research 55, 58
    theoretical, methodological,
        analytical and stylistic
        adequacy 70–71
    useful considerations 22
Research Fellows 3, 10
research grants 4, 22
    research funding proposal
        (RFP) 58–60
    seeking funding 57–58
    writing applications 123–24
research uptake 113–15
ResearchGate 114, 115, 130
roundtables 100

scholarship of teaching and learning
    (SoTL) 41, 122
self-plagiarism 63
self-publishing 71
seminars 98–99, 105, 106

Senior Tutors 3
service 3, 4, 91
   coaching 29
   collegiality 93
   community service 92, 96–97
   departmental or institutional
      level 93–94
   description 92
   disciplinary level 94–95
   goals 21, 22
   leadership 124–25
   mentoring 29
   professional level 95–96
   sponsoring 29
   useful considerations 21–22
SNIP (Source Normalized Impact per
   Paper) 113
social commenting 119
social media 115, 116
sponsoring, academic 28, 29
standards, academic 3–4
students
   see also supervision; teaching
   help with problems 131
   managing queries 131
summative assignments 39–40
supervision 4, 21, 28, 40, 41, 80, 133
   dealing with issues 87
   examining theses and
      dissertations 88–90
   expectations of a supervisor 83–85
   importance 81–82
   leadership 122–23
   mentoring 122
   personal and professional
      benefits 82–83
   students from diverse
      backgrounds 86–87
   supervisors as authors 76
symposia 100

teaching 3, 4, 9
   academic skill development 45–46
   coaching 29
   culturally responsive teaching 48–51
   deciding whether to accept
      opportunities 18–19
   differences between undergraduate
      and postgraduate teaching 47
   gaining experience 42–43, 128–29
   goals 22
   innovative formats 51–53
   leadership 122–23
   mentoring 27, 29, 122
   portfolio 40–41, 109, 110
   postgraduate teaching 46–48
   preparation 42–43, 44
   sponsoring 29
   undergraduate teaching 43–45, 47
   useful considerations 21
Teaching and Learning Research
   Initiative 124
teaching assistants 32, 40, 41, 122
teaching awards 21, 41, 109, 110
   portfolio 110
technology
   dissemination of ideas and
      research 115–16
   in teaching 51–53
tenure, making the most of prior
   time 105–06
tertiary institutions 3
   see also polytechnics
theses and dissertations
   see also supervision
   examining 88–90
   recommendations 55, 56, 117
   statement describing a thesis 55, 58
   turning a thesis into a book 71–73
time management 52, 128, 130–33

Tuākana programme 50
tutoring 9, 41
   preparation 33–34
   preparation of students
      for assignments and
      examinations 37–39
   preparing a portfolio 40–41
   reasons for undertaking
      tutoring 32–33
   Senior Tutors 3
   sense making 35–36
   structuring a tutorial 36–37
   student engagement 34–35
Twitter 116

vanity publishing 71

wānanga 48
Web of Science 113, 114
websites 115–16, 117
whakamana 49
whanaungatanga 49
women academics 14
work experience, recognition in place of
    qualifications 3
work–life balance 2, 23, 133–35
workload 1–2, 127–29, 132, 133
   see also time management
   where to go for help with
      difficulties 135–37
workshops 101
writing
   see also publications
   abstracts 64
   city—suburb—street structure for
     essays and exam questions 45–46
   deadlines 136
   deciding whether to accept
     opportunities 18–19, 24
   essays and assignments 37–39, 45
   keeping up momentum 66–68
   maximising earlier work 61–63
   research grant applications 123–24
   style 45, 90
   writing plan 64–66

YouTube clips 116, 117

www.ingramcontent.com/pod-product-compliance
Lightning Source LLC
Chambersburg PA
CBHW080807300426
44114CB00020B/2857